ORTHODOX

OF THE

BRITISH ISLES

VOLUME ONE
JANUARY – MARCH

JOHN (ELLSWORTH) HUTCHISON-HALL BA (HONS) LTH DMIN

Published in association with St. Eadfrith Press

Printed in the United States of America

Publisher's Cataloguing-in-Publication data

Hutchison-Hall, John (Ellsworth).
    Orthodox Saints of the British Isles - Volume I: January – March.
p. cm.
        Includes   bibliographical
references and index
        ISBN-13: 978-0615925806
        ISBN-10: 0615925804
1. Christian saints—Biography.

I. Hutchison-Hall, John (Ellsworth). II john-that-
theologian.com. III. Title.

Library of Congress Control Number: 2013921550
BX4655.3.H88 2013
282'.092'2—dc22

INTERCESSION TO ALL THE SAINTS OF ENGLAND

O GOD, Save thy People and Bless Thine Inheritance, Visit Thy World with Mercies and Bounties. Exalt the Horn of Orthodox Christians and Send Down upon us Thy Rich Mercies. Through the Prayers of Our Most Pure Lady, the Mother of God and Ever-Virgin Mary; through the Might of the Precious and Life-Giving Cross; through the Protection of the Heavenly Bodiless Hosts, through the Protection of the Honourable, Glorious Prophet, Forerunner and Baptist John; of the Holy, Glorious and All-Praised Chiefs of the Apostles, Peter and Paul, of the Holy Apostles Simon the Zealot and Aristobulus and all the Twelve and Seventy Holy Apostles; of our Holy Fathers, Great Hierarchs and Universal Teachers, Basil the Great, Gregory the Theologian and John Chrysostom; of our Holy Father, Nicholas, Archbishop of Myra in Lycia, The Wonderworker; of the Holy Martyr Alban the First Martyr of the Islands; of our Holy Fathers Gregory the Great and Augustine of Canterbury, Apostles of the English, Ethelbert, High King of the English, Laurence and Mellitus, Archbishops of Canterbury, Oswald of Heavenfield, Paulinus of York, Felix of Dunwich, Apostle of East Anglia, Aidan of Lindisfarne, Birinus and Cedd, Apostles of Wessex and Essex, Botolph of Iken, Chad of Lichfield, Cuthbert of Lindisfarne, the Wonderworker; of our Holy Mothers, Audrey of Ely, Hilda of Whitby, Mildred of Minster, Werburgh of Chester, Milburgh of Wenlock; of our Holy Fathers, Theodore of Tarsus, Archbishop of Canterbury, Erkenwald, the Light of

London, Benedict of Wearmouth, Wilfrid of York, Aldhelm of Sherborne, Guthlac of Crowland, Bede the Venerable, Clement and Boniface, Apostles to the Heathen; Swithin of Winchester, the Wonder-worker, Edmund the Martyr, King of East Anglia, Theodore of Crowland and all those Cruelly Martyred by the Northmen; of the Holy King of England, Edgar the Peaceful, of the Holy, Right-Believing King of England and Passion-Bearer Edward the Martyr; of our Holy Mother Edith of Wilton; of our Holy Fathers Ethelwold of Winchester, Dunstan of Canterbury, Oswald of York, Alphege the Martyr, Archbishop of Canterbury, of the Holy and Righteous New Martyr Elizabeth and the Newly-Revealed John, Archbishop in London, and of all the Saints who have Shone Forth in the English Land; of the Holy, Victorious George the Great-Martyr; of the Holy, Glorious Martyrs and all the New Martyrs and Confessors of all the Lands of the Earth; of our Reverend and God-Bearing Fathers, the Holy and Righteous Ancestors of God, Joachim and Anne; and of all Thy Saints, we Beseech Thee, O Most Merciful Lord, Hearken unto the Petitions of us Sinners who Make our Supplications unto Thee, and Have Mercy upon us.

To my children, Iain and Alexandra, with much love.
Through the prayers of the Saints of our ancestral
land may God grant you many years.

INTRODUCTION

*"The Church in The British Isles will only begin to grow when
She begins to again venerate Her own Saints"
(St. Arsenios of Paros † A.D. 1877)*

As I approached my baptism and chrismation into the Orthodox Church,
I faced the prospect of choosing a patron saint. Though I generally go by
Ellsworth, my given names are William Ellsworth Henry. I knew there
was no chance there was a St. Ellsworth, but, due to the Slavo-centrism of
my wonderful priest and my own ignorance, I did not know there was an
Orthodox, albeit Western, St. William or a St. Henry. No information
was available to support my first choice of St. Augustine of Canterbury.
So I asked my priest if there was an Orthodox equivalent to *Butler's Lives of
the Saints**; he told me about the *Prologue of Ohrid*, but that it wasn't
available in English.

In the ensuing decade and a half, including several years spent in a
monastery, I served as a chaplain, and earned graduate degrees in theology
and ministry. About two years ago as I was looking at the Church
calendar I came across SS. Tancred, Torthred and Tova (30th September),
and not recognising them decided to look them up. After several
frustrating hours of research I finally found some information about them;
I realised there had to be a better way. The result is this first volume of a
series of books on the lives of Orthodox western saints, my blog, and the
Western Saints section of my website.

I started with the saints of the British Isles simply because of my ancestry
and Anglophilia. The volumes on the saints of the Continent are not far
behind and their lives are just as wonderful, and inspiring to learn about.

We are now very fortunate to have available to us the *Prologue of Ohrid* in
English. However, there is still a dearth of easily accessible information on

the lives of Orthodox Western Saints. My goal in writing this book is to create a "Butler's-meets-Prologue" if you will.

Divine Providence led me to choose St. John of Shanghai and San Francisco as my patron and I could not have selected a better role model. I shall end this introduction with the wise words of Vladika:

> "Never, never, never let anyone tell you that, in order to be Orthodox, you must also be eastern.
> The West was Orthodox for a thousand years, and her venerable liturgy is far older than any of her heresies."

A FEW NOTES:

The dates in this book correspond to the Church calendar. If the reader uses the Revised Julian or "New" Calendar then the dates will coincide with the civil date. For those readers who follow the traditional Julian or "Old" Calendar, the dates in this book are thirteen days behind the civil calendar i.e. the listing for 1st January in this book corresponds to 14th January civil date.

Throughout the text, an asterisk* is used to denote a term or name explained more completely in Appendix I.

Acknowledgments

So many people have been instrumental in getting me through the process of researching and writing this book, that I hardly know where to start.

Thanks to:

My son Iain for his enthusiasm and encouragement.

My dearest friend Jennifer Bronwyn Leigh, *éditrice extraordinaire*, who took an informative text and made it enjoyable to read as well.

My dear friends Mary Lou and Margaret who have been big supporters of this project.

Kolina who has taught me more about Photoshop than she will ever realise.

Destiny for her help with the cover.

Too many hours have been spent in Starbucks stores #11649 and #14841; and I must give special thanks to the managers and staff (past and present) who have kept me well supplied with tea, hot water, the occasional pastry, and many smiles and words of encouragement as I've worked.

And last, but not least, The Fluffernut Gang.

TABLE OF CONTENTS

Intercession to All the Saints of England iii

Introduction vii

A Few Notes: viii

Acknowledgments ix

Table of Contents xi

1st January 23

    Connat (Comnatan) 23

    Cuan (Mochua, Moncan) 23

    Elvan and Mydwyn 23

    Fanchea (Garbh) 24

    Maelrhys 24

2nd January 25

    Munchin 25

3rd January 27

    Finlugh (Finlag) 27

    Fintan 27

    Wenog 27

4th January 29

5th January 31

    Cera (Ciar, Cyra, Cior, Ceara) 31

    Kiara (Chier) 31

6th January 33

    Diman (Dimas, Dima) 33

    Eigrad 33

Hywyn 33

Merinus 33

Peter of Canterbury 34

Schotin (Scarthin) 34

7th January 35

Brannoc 35

Cronan Beg 36

Kentigerna 36

8th January 37

Albert of Cashel 37

Athelhelm (Athelm) 37

Ergnad (Ercnacta) 37

Nathalan 38

Pega 38

Wulsin 39

9th January 41

Brithwald (Berethwald, Brihtwald) 41

Foellan (Foilan, Fillan) 41

10th January 43

Dermot (Diarmis, Diarmaid) 43

Thomian (Toimen) 43

11th January 45

Ethenia and Fidelmia 45

12th January 47

Benedict Biscop 47

13th January 49

Elian (Eilan, Allan) 49

Elian ap Erbin 49

Eloan 50

Erbin (Ervan, Erbyn, Erme or Hermes) 50

Kentigern Mungo 50

14th January 53

Deusdedit 53

15th January 55

Blaithmaic (Blathmac, Blaithmale) 55

Ceolwulf 55

Ita (Ida, Ytha, Meda) 55

Lleudadd (Laudatus) 56

Sawl 57

16th January 59

Dunchaid O'Braoin 59

Fursey (Fursæus) 59

17th January 61

Mildgyth 61

Nennius 61

18th January 63

19th January 65

Branwallader 65

20th January 67

Fechin 67

Molagga (Laicin) 67

21st January 69

Brigid (Briga) 69

Lawdog 69

Vimin (Wynnin, Gwynnin).. 69

Wilgils 70

22nd January 71

Brithwald 71

23rd January 73

Colman of Lismore 73

24th January 75

Cadoc (Docus, Cathmael, Cadvaci)................................... 75

Guasacht 76

25th January 77

Dwynwen 77

Eochod (Euchadius) 77

Sigebert 77

Thorgyth (Tortgith) 78

26th January 79

Conan 79

27th January 81

Natalis (Naile) 81

28th January 83

Cannera (Cainder, Kinnera) 83

Glastian (Glastianus, Mac-Glastian) 83

29th January 85

Blath (Flora) 85

Dallán Forgaill (of Cluain Dallain)................................... 85

Voloc 85

30th January 87

Tudy (Tudclyd, Tybie, Tydie)... 87

31ˢᵗ January 89

    Adamnan 89

    Áedan (Aidan, Máedóc) 89

    Madoes (Madianus) 90

1ˢᵗ February 91

    Brigid (Bridget, Bride) 91

    Cinnia 93

    Crewenna 93

    Darlugdach (Dardulacha, Derlugdach) 93

    Jarlath (Hierlath) 94

    Kinnia 94

    Seiriol 94

2ⁿᵈ February 95

    Feock 95

    Laurence of Canterbury 95

3ʳᵈ February 97

    Caellainn (Caoilfionn) 97

    Ia (Hia, Ives) 97

    Werburg (Werburgh) 97

    Werburgh 98

4ᵗʰ February 99

    Aldate 99

    Liephard 99

    Modan 100

5ᵗʰ February 101

    Indract 101

6ᵗʰ February 103

Mel (Melchno) 103

Mun.. 103

7th February 105

Augulus (Augurius, Aule) 105

Richard 105

8th February 107

Cuthman.. 107

Elfleda (Ælflæd) 107

Kigwe (Kewe, Ciwa) 107

Oncho (Onchuo) 108

9th February 109

Cronan the Wise 109

Cuaran (Curvinus, Cronan)............................... 109

Eingan (Einion, Eneon, Anianus) 109

Teio (Teilio, Teilus, Thelian, Teilan, Teiou, Teliou, Dillo, Dillon)... 110

10th February 111

Merewenna 111

Trumwin 111

11th February 113

Cædmon 113

Gobnata (Gobnet) 114

12th February 117

Ethilwold.. 117

13th February 119

Dyfnog.. 119

Ermenhild (Ermengild, Ermenilda)................... 119

Huna 119

Modomnock (Domnoc, Dominic)...................................... 120

14th February 121

    Conran 121

15th February 123

    Berach (Barachias, Berachius) 123

    Dochow (Dochau, Dogwyn) 123

    Farannan 123

16th February 125

17th February 127

    Finan 127

    Fintan 128

    Fortchern 128

    Loman (Luman) 128

18th February 129

    Colman of Lindisfarne 129

    Ethelina (Eudelme) 130

19th February 131

    Odran 131

20th February 133

    Bolcan (Olcan) 133

    Colgan 133

21st February 135

22nd February 137

    Elwin 137

    John the Saxon 137

23rd February 139

    Boswell (Boisil) 139

Milburgh (Milburga or Mildburh) 139

24th February 141

Cumine the White 141

Liudhard (Letard) 141

25th February 143

Ethelbert (Albert) of Kent 143

26th February 145

27th February 147

Alnoth 147

Comgan 147

Herefrith 147

28th February 149

Llibio 149

Maidoc (Madoc) 149

Oswald 149

Sillan (Silvanus) 150

1st March 151

David 151

Marnock (Marnanus, Marnan, Marnoc) 152

Monan 152

2nd March 153

Chad (Ceadda) 153

Cynibil (Cynibild) 154

Fergna 154

Gistilian (Gistlian) 154

Slebhene (Slebhine) 155

3rd March 157

Cele-Christ 157

Foila (Faile, Foilenna, Fallena) 157

Lamalisse 157

Non (Nonna, Nonnita) 157

Winwaloe 158

4th March 159

Adrian and Companions 159

Owen 159

5th March 161

Caron 161

Carthage the Elder 161

Colman of Armagh 161

Kieran (Kieman, Kyran, Ciaran) 161

Piran (Pyran) 162

6th March 163

Baldred (Balther) 163

Bilfrid (Billfrith) 163

Cyneburgh, Cyneswith and Tibba 163

7th March 165

Deifer 165

Enodoch (Wenedoc) 165

Eosterwine 165

8th March 167

Beoadh (Beatus) 167

Felix of Dunwich 167

Rhian (Ranus, Rian) 168

Senan (Senames) 169

9th March 171

    Bosa 171

    Constantine 171

10th March 173

    Failbhe the Little 173

    Kessog (Mackessog) 173

    Sedna 173

    Silvester 173

11th March 175

    Ængus (Angus) 175

12th March 177

    Alphege the Elder 177

    Mura McFeredach (Muran, Murames) 177

13th March 179

    Gerald 179

    Kevoca (Kennotha, Quivoca) 179

    Mochoemoc (Mochaemhog, Pulcherius, Vulcanius) 179

14th March 181

    Boniface Curitan 181

    Talmach 181

15th March 183

16th March 185

    Abban 185

    Finian 185

17th March 187

    Patrick 187

18th March 191

Edward the Martyr 191

Egbert 193

19th March 195

Alcmund 195

Auxilius 195

Lactan 195

20th March 197

Cuthbert 197

Herbert 199

21st March 201

Enda (Endeus, Enna) 201

22nd March 203

Darerca 203

Failbhe 203

Trien (Trienan) 203

23rd March 205

Ethilwald 205

Maidoc (Mo-Mhaedog) 205

24th March 207

Caimin (Cammin) of Inniskeltra 207

Cairlon (Caorlan) 207

Domangard (Donard) 207

Macartan (Macartin, Maccarthen) 208

25th March 209

Alfwold (Ælfwold) 209

Kennocha (Kyle, Enoch) 209

26th March 211

Garbhan 211

Mochelloc (Cellog, Mottelog, Motalogus) 211

Sincheall 211

27th March 213

Alkeld (Athilda) 213

Suairlech 213

28th March 215

29th March 217

Gladys 217

Gwynllyw (Woollos) 217

Lasar (Lassar, Lassera) 217

30th March 219

Fergus 219

Osburgh (Osburga) 219

Tola 219

31st March 221

Appendix – I 223

Appendix – II – Decree on the Veneration of Ancient Saints of the West
.... 231

Bibliography/References 233

Index 237

1ˢᵀ January

Connat (Comnatan) – Sixth Century

The successor of St. Brigid (21ˢᵗ January) as the Abbess of Kildare, she served in this role until her repose circa A.D. 590. There is no further information on St. Connat extant.

Cuan (Mochua, Moncan) – Sixth Century

After being educated by St. Comgall (10ᵗʰ May) at Bangor Abbey, he founded a monastery at Gael. He travelled to Fore, then Hy-Many in the country of Connaught. He went on to found the diocese and abbey of Balla, Co. Mayo, Ireland in A.D. 616, serving as its first abbot-bishop. A tireless Wonder-worker, and confessor of the faith, he lived to be nearly 100, founding many other churches and monasteries throughout Ireland.

Elvan and Mydwyn – Second Century

Elvan and Mydwyn are traditionally believed to have been two Britons who were sent by King St. Lucius (3ʳᵈ December) to Pope St. Eleutherius to ask for missionaries. Unfortunately there is no record extant regarding these Saints, hence we are left with unsupported, and perhaps unreliable legends alluded to by St. Bede the Venerable (25ᵗʰ May) and repeated by Butler*, for evidence of their existence.

FANCHEA (GARBH) — SIXTH CENTURY

Foundress of a convent at Rossory in Fermanagh, St. Fanchea was a daughter of Conall the Red prince of Oriel, in Ulster, and his wife Briga, and sister of St. Enda (21ˢᵗ March). St. Fanchea was instrumental in her brother's decision to embrace monastic life. Reposing towards the end of the sixth century A.D., she was buried in Killane.

MAELRHYS — SIXTH CENTURY

A sixth century saint of the Isle of Bardsey in Wales, he was probably born in Brittany. Nothing further is known.

2ND JANUARY

MUNCHIN — SEVENTH CENTURY ?

Mainchín mac Setnai (anglicised to Munchin) is believed to have been the first Bishop of Limerick, Ireland, though this is debated. He is also the patron saint of Limerick, along with St. Ita (15th January).

3RD JANUARY

FINLUGH (FINLAG) — SIXTH CENTURY

A Brother of St. Fintan *(vide infra)*, St. Finlugh left his native Ireland. He travelled to Scotland where it is thought he became a disciple of St. Columba of Iona (9th June). He later returned to Ireland to serve as abbot of a monastery founded by St. Columba of Iona in Co. Derry.

FINTAN — SIXTH CENTURY

St. Fintan was a brother of St. Finlugh *(vide supra)*, who was a disciple of St. Comgall (10th May) at Bangor. He is the patron saint of Doon in Ireland where his holy well still exists.

WENOG — DATE UNKNOWN

St. Wenog was an early Welsh saint about whom there is no information extant.

4ᵀᴴ JANUARY

There are no Saints of the British Isles listed on the Calendar for this date.

5ᵀᴴ JANUARY

CERA (CIAR, CYRA, CIOR, CEARA) – SEVENTH CENTURY

St. Cera was a native of Tipperary who founded and was abbess of two convents, one at Kilkeary and the other at Tech Telle (Tehelly). There is no further reliable information on this saint extant, and she is sometimes confused with St. Kiara (Chier) *(following entry)*.

KIARA (CHIER) – SEVENTH CENTURY

A spiritual daughter of St. Fintan Munnu (21ˢᵗ October), she lived in North Tipperary at a place now named Kilkeary in her honour. St. Kiara reposed circa A.D. 680; there is no further information extant.

6TH January

DIMAN (DIMAS, DIMA) — SEVENTH CENTURY

A monk under St. Columba of Iona (9th June), and later Bishop of Connor in Ireland, St. Diman reposed A.D. 658. He was one of the prelates to whom the Church in Rome addressed its epistle on the Paschal Controversy* and on the errors of Pelagianism*.

EIGRAD — SIXTH CENTURY

A brother of St. Samson (28th July), he was a disciple of St. Illtyd (6th November) and founder of a church at Anglesey in Wales.

HYWYN — SIXTH CENTURY

St. Hywyn was most likely a companion of St. Cadfan (1st November) on his return journey from Brittany to Cornwall and Wales A.D. 516. It is believed that he was the founder of Aberdaron (Carnarvon); in addition, there are several churches in the West of England known as St. Owen's or St. Ewen's, which may have him for their patron. There are no other details of his life extant.

MERINUS — SIXTH CENTURY

St. Merinus was a disciple of St. Donat (Dunwyd) (7th August) of Bangor, and patron saint of churches in Wales and in Brittany. He lived at some point in the sixth century A.D.; there is no further information on this saint extant.

PETER OF CANTERBURY — SEVENTH CENTURY

A member of the Gregorian mission to the Anglo-Saxons, St. Peter was the first Abbot of the monastery (SS. Peter and Paul — later St. Augustine's) founded by St. Augustine of Canterbury (27th May). St. Peter was killed at Ambleteuse, near Boulogne either A.D. 607 or A.D. 614. His relics are still honoured at the location of his repose.

SCHOTIN (SCARTHIN) — SIXTH CENTURY

Whilst still quite young, this saint left his native Ireland to become a disciple of St. David (1st March) in Wales. He later returned to Ireland, living as a hermit on Mt. Mairge in Leix for many years, he was also the founder of a school for youths at Kilkenny.

7TH JANUARY

BRANNOC — SIXTH CENTURY

A sixth century saint, legends concerning him vary and are unreliable. However, it seems that he served for a time as tutor to the children of King St. Brychan of Brycheiniog (6th April), and accompanied the king on a pilgrimage to venerate the tombs of the Apostles, possibly stopping in Brittany on his return for several years. Returning to Britain, he founded a monastery at Braughton, near Barnstaple in Devon, where his relics are said to rest beneath the church altar.

CRONAN BEG — SEVENTH CENTURY

A Bishop of Ændrum, Co. Down, Ireland, St. Cronan Beg is mentioned in connexion with the Paschal Controversy in A.D. 640. There is no further information extant.

KENTIGERNA — EIGHTH CENTURY

St. Kentigerna was the mother of St. Coellan (29th July) and the daughter of Kelly, Prince of Leinster, Ireland. Upon the death of her husband, she left Ireland and moved to Inchebroida Island in Loch Lomond, Scotland, where, along with her brother St. Comgan (13th October) and her son St. Foellan (9th January), she lived as an anchoress until her repose A.D. 733. A church remains dedicated to her to this day.

8TH JANUARY

ALBERT OF CASHEL — SEVENTH CENTURY

Whilst no reliable Life of this saint is extant, it seems that he was born in England and evangelised in Ireland and then later in Bavaria with St. Erard. He went on a pilgrimage to Jerusalem and, on his return to Bavaria, reposed, and was buried in Regensburg. St. Albert is the patron saint of Cashel in Ireland.

ATHELHELM (ATHELM) — TENTH CENTURY

The twenty-first Archbishop of Canterbury, and an uncle of St. Dunstan (19th May). St. Athelhelm was a monk, and later became Abbot of Glastonbury. He was consecrated the first Bishop of Wells in Somerset A.D. 909, serving that See until his elevation to the Archbishopric of Canterbury in A.D. 923, reposing shortly after his elevation to that See. Some sources claim he reposed A.D. 926 and most likely presided at the coronation of King Athelstan of England A.D. 925, though there is no definitive evidence to support this.

ERGNAD (ERCNACTA) — FIFTH CENTURY

A native of present-day Antrim, this holy woman is said to have been tonsured by St. Patrick (17th March). She spent her monastic life as an anchoress and her last years were marked by many miracles.

TROPARION OF ST. ERGNAD TONE 3

Turning thy back on the transitory glamour of the world, O Mother Ergnad,
thou wast tonsured by the Hierarch Patrick.
By fulfilling thy obedience, thou dost teach us the virtue of humility.
Wherefore, O righteous one, pray that we may be given grace
to accept spiritual guidance for the salvation of our souls.

KONTAKION OF ST. ERGNAD TONE 8

Adornment of Ireland and joy of monastics, O Mother Ergnad
thou didst trample on the fiery passions, which war against the soul.
O conqueror of them all and champion of purity,
we praise thee, as is thy due, and in thine honour, we sing: Alleluia.

NATHALAN — SEVENTH CENTURY

Born to a wealthy landed family in Scotland, St. Nathalan distributed his
estate amongst the poor and became a hermit, combining tilling the soil
with assiduous prayer. He was famous for his learning (both secular and
sacred), and his zeal in spreading the Faith. Elevated to the Bishopric of
Aberdeen, he continued his charity to the poor, living in great austerity.
St. Nathalan reposed A.D. 679.

PEGA — EIGHTH CENTURY

St. Pega was the sister of St. Guthlac (11th April), who also lived an
hermetic life, initially at Crowland and then finally in Northamptonshire,
where the village of Peakirk (Pega's church) commemorates her. At some
point after St. Guthlac's repose, St. Pega went to Rome where she reposed
circa A.D. 719. Her relics were placed in a local church, the name of

which is now lost to us; however, they were reportedly the source of many miracles.

WULSIN — TENTH CENTURY

St. Wulsin was a monk and one of the restorers of monastic discipline in England during the tenth century A.D. under St. Dunstan (19th May). Appointed to serve as superior over the restored community at Westminster circa A.D. 960, he was elevated to Abbot A.D. 980. St. Wulsin was consecrated Bishop of Sherborne which he served until his repose A.D. 1002.

9TH JANUARY

BRITHWALD (BERETHWALD, BRIHTWALD) — EIGHTH CENTURY

Of Anglo-Saxon ancestry, the ninth Archbishop of Canterbury began as a monk and then became Abbot of Glastonbury. He resigned that dignity to devote his life to study and prayer at the small monastery of Reculver, near the Isle of Thanet in Kent. Upon the death of St. Theodore of Canterbury (19th September), A.D. 692, he was elevated to the Archbishopric of Canterbury; serving that See until his repose A.D. 731.

FOELLAN (FOILAN, FILLAN) — EIGHTH CENTURY

After accompanying his mother, St. Kentigerna (7th January), and uncle, St. Comgan (13th October) from their native Ireland to Scotland, St. Foellan embraced the monastic life and laboured as a missionary until he was quite advanced in years. The place of his repose is called Strathfillan after him.

10TH JANUARY

DERMOT (DIARMIS, DIARMAID) — SIXTH CENTURY

Known from his earliest years for his sanctity, he was the spiritual father
and teacher of St. Kieran of Clonmacnoise (9th September). St. Dermot
went on to found, and serve as first abbot of a monastery on Innis-Clotran
Island (Inchcleraun), Co. Longford Ireland.

THOMIAN (TOIMEN) — SEVENTH CENTURY

St. Thomian was the seventeenth Archbishop of Armagh, from circa A.D.
623 until circa A.D. 660. Always renowned for his great sanctity of life, he
is also remembered for a letter he wrote to Rome concerning the Paschal
Controversy.

11TH JANUARY

ETHENIA AND FIDELMIA — FIFTH CENTURY

Amongst the first converts of St. Patrick (17th March), they were daughters of King Laoghaire. Following their conversion, they became nuns and reposed in holiness A.D. 433.

KONTAKION OF SS. ETHENIA AND FIDELMIA TONE 4

Having been tonsured, O most pure and righteous virgins Ethenia and Fidelmia,
you were found worthy to tarry in this vale of tears
and to receive the Body and Blood of Christ, just once,
before going to your eternal reward.
We chant your praises and implore Christ our God
that, in The Eleventh Day of Judgment,
He will not find us wanting.

12TH January

BENEDICT BISCOP — SEVENTH CENTURY

St. Benedict Biscop was a Northumbrian of noble birth, who spent his youth at the court of King Oswiu. Returning from his second pilgrimage to Rome, A.D. 666, he became a monk at Lérins. Three years later, he accompanied St. Theodore (19th September) to Canterbury, where he became Abbot of the monastery of SS. Peter and Paul (later St. Augustine's). He went on to found the monasteries of St. Peter at Wearmouth (A.D. 674) and St. Paul at Jarrow (A.D. 682). St. Benedict was an ardent advocate of Roman liturgical practice, and was well known for his enthusiasm for art and learning, returning from each of his five trips to Rome with numerous paintings, relics, and manuscripts. He was responsible for bringing John the Archcantor of St. Peter's in Rome to England to teach Roman chant, and is said to have introduced the use of glass windows and stone in the construction of English churches. St. Benedict's Life was written by St. Bede the Venerable (25th May), who was St. Benedict's charge from the age of seven.

13ᵀᴴ JANUARY

ELIAN (EILAN, ALLAN) – SIXTH CENTURY

He is believed to have been born in Cornwall, and was a member of the family of St. Ismael (16ᵗʰ June). The towns of Llanelian in Anglesey and Llanelian in Clwyd are named in his honour, and St. Allen's church in Cornwall is dedicated to him.

ELIAN AP ERBIN – FIFTH CENTURY

There are no certain details on this saint extant, aside from his appearance on some Welsh Calendars. It is possible that he is the same saint as the St.

Eloan, another fifth century A.D. saint, whose Feast is also kept on 12th January.

ELOAN — FIFTH CENTURY

There is no information on this saint extant, and it is quite possible that he is the same as St. Elian ap Erbin, another fifth century A.D. saint, whose Feast is also kept on 12th January (*vide supra*).

ERBIN (ERVAN, ERBYN, ERME OR HERMES) — FIFTH CENTURY

Erbin was a Cornish saint, who most likely lived in the fifth century A.D. There are churches dedicated to him and his name appears in several Calendars. It appears that he was related to one of the Cornish or Devonian chieftains of his time. For reasons unknown, his name has sometimes been spelled *Hermes*, confusing him with the ancient martyr of that name.

KENTIGERN MUNGO — SIXTH CENTURY

Our father among the Saints Kentigern of Glasgow (in Latin: Cantigernus and in Welsh: Cyndeyrn Garthwys or Kyndeyrn), also known as St. Mungo, was a late sixth century A.D. missionary to the Brythonic Kingdom of Strathclyde. St. Kentigern is venerated as the Apostle of what is now northwest England (including Cumbria and the Lake District) and southwest Scotland, and is a patron saint of Glasgow.

What we know of this saint comes from a twelfth century Life, which is of questionable reliability. It seems he was a grandson of a British prince in Southern Scotland, and raised by St. Serf (1st July) in a monastic school at Culross on the Firth of Forth. He was consecrated the first Bishop of the Britons of Strathclyde and founded the Church of Glasgow. Driven from Strathclyde by persecution, he went to Wales, where he is believed to have founded St. Asaph monastery, and then to Cumbria. He eventually returned to Strathclyde where he reposed A.D. 612; his reputed tomb stands in the cathedral.

14TH JANUARY

DEUSDEDIT — SEVENTH CENTURY

A native of Wessex, whose Saxon name was Frithona, and of whose early life nothing is known. He succeeded St. Honorius to the See of Canterbury in A.D. 655, becoming the first Anglo-Saxon to serve as Primate. The consecration of Damian as Bishop of Rochester in A.D. 656 is the sole official act of his that is known with absolute certainty. St. Deusdedit reposed a casualty of the Great Pestilence of A.D. 664.

15TH JANUARY

BLAITHMAIC (BLATHMAC, BLAITHMALE) — NINTH CENTURY

The son of an Irish king, who at an early age renounced this world and entered the monastic life, St. Blaithmaic ultimately became abbot of his monastery. He later led a group of monks to reclaim Iona*, where he was martyred, circa A.D. 823, by Vikings on the altar steps of the church for refusing to identify the tomb of St. Columba of Iona (9th June) which they sought to plunder. His Life was written in verse by Strabo, the Abbot of Reichenau in Lake Constance in southern present-day Germany.

CEOLWULF — EIGHTH CENTURY

A King of Northumbria and great supporter of monasticism, he abdicated his throne A.D. 737 to enter Lindisfarne. St. Bede the Venerable (25th May) dedicated his *Ecclesiastical History* to him. St. Ceolwulf reposed A.D. 764.

ITA (IDA, YTHA, MEDA) — SIXTH CENTURY

Second only to St. Brigid (1st February) in veneration amongst the Irish, St. Ita is known as "the Foster mother of Irish Saints". The daughter of Irish nobility, whose parents were devout Christians, St. Ita resolved, while still quite young, to enter monastic life. She founded a school and monastery at Killeedy (Cill Íde) in present-day Co. Waterford, which became known as a training ground for young boys, many of whom became famous churchmen, including St. Brendan the Voyager (16th May), who was entrusted to her care at the age of one, remaining with her for five years. She spent her life in repentance and practicing asceticism and became a renowned elderess, widely sought for her spiritual counsel. She seems to have practiced medicine to some extent as well.

St. Ita reposed circa A.D. 570, and is the patron saint of Killeedy. There is a holy well on the spot of her monastery, which is a site of pilgrimage.

LLEUDADD (LAUDATUS) — SIXTH CENTURY

St. Lleudadd was a Welsh saint about whom there is little reliable information. He was Abbot of Bardsey (Carnarvon) at some point, and is said to have accompanied St. Cadfan (1st November) to Brittany. There are some who are of the opinion that he is the same saint as St. Lo of Coutances, though in the absence of a reliable Life or other details, it is impossible to say with any certainty.

SAWL — SIXTH CENTURY

A Welsh chieftain, St. Sawl was father of St. Asaph of Wales (1ˢᵗ May). There is no other information on this saint extant.

16TH JANUARY

DUNCHAID O'BRAOIN — TENTH CENTURY

A native of Westmeath in Ireland, he was an anchorite near the monastery of Clonmacnoise until A.D. 969, when he became their abbot. It is believed that St. Dunchaid O'Braoin returned to the hermetic life for the last few years before reposing A.D. 988.

FURSEY (FURSÆUS) — SEVENTH CENTURY

St. Fursey was an Irish monk who did much to establish Christianity throughout the British Isles, particularly in East Anglia. The son of St. Fintan, and grandson of Finlog, pagan king of the area, his mother was Gelges, the Christian daughter of Áed-Finn, king of Connaught. He was most likely baptized by St. Brendan the Voyager (16th May), his father's uncle, and later educated by St. Brendan's monks. St. Fursey was tonsured at Inisquin (near Galway) and devoted himself to monastic life. He later built his own monastery at Rathmat, (according to St. Bede the Venerable (25th May) this was inspired by a vision he had) in the Diocese of Tuam, now Kill-Fursa, serving as its first abbot. In time, his brothers SS. Foillan (9th January) and Ultan (2nd May) joined the community at Rathmat, though by this point St. Fursey seems to have renounced the administration of the monastery, and devoted himself to preaching throughout the area, as well as the frequent exorcism of evil spirits.

Around A.D. 633, he, along with his brothers SS. Foillan (9th January) and Ultan (2nd May), travelled to East Anglia. There he was received by King St. Sigebert (25th January), who gave him a tract of land at Cnobheresburg on which he built a monastery within the enclosure of a Roman fort — Burghcastle in Suffolk — surrounded by woods and overlooking the sea. Here he laboured for several years converting the Picts and Saxons. He also tonsured King St. Sigebert into the monastic state. Once again, he sought the hermetic life and withdrew with St. Ultan to live as an anchorite. About a year later war threatened East Anglia, and St. Fursey disbanded his monks and sailed with his brothers and six other monks to Gaul, arriving in Normandy in A.D. 648. Once there, through the generosity of Clovis II, he built the great monastery of Lagny, approximately 25 km east of the present centre of Paris. At one point St. Fursey was deputed by the Bishop of Paris to govern his Diocese as his vicar general, which has led to some describing him as a Bishop himself.

St. Fursey reposed A.D. 650 at Froheins (Fursei-domus), whilst he was building another monastery at Peronne. His relics have been famous for miracles, and are still preserved in the great church at Peronne. St. Fursey is the patron saint of Peronne, and patron saint of the Parish of Headford.

17TH JANUARY

MILDGYTH — SEVENTH CENTURY

St. Mildgyth was the youngest and least well known of the three daughters of Merewald, King of Mercia, and Ermenburga, Princess of Kent. Along with her sisters, SS. Mildred (13th July) and Milburgh (23rd February), St. Mildgyth entered monastic life. After receiving monastic tonsure at Eastry Monastery, she joined her sisters at Minster-in-Thanet, and upon at St. Mildred's death succeeded her as abbess. St. Mildgyth reposed circa A.D. 676.

NENNIUS — SIXTH CENTURY

No details of this saint survive to this day, though he is mentioned in the Lives of several other saints. He was a member of the Irish nobility who forsook his high-born life for the monastery. He began under St. Fiace of Leinster (12th October), and later moved on to Clonard as a disciple of St. Finian (12th December). He is counted as one of the 'Twelve Apostles of Ireland'.

18TH JANUARY

There are no Saints of the British Isles listed on the Calendar for this date.

19TH JANUARY

BRANWALLADER — SIXTH CENTURY?

Branwallader (also Branwalader, Branwalator, Breward and Brelade: it is also likely that "St. Brelade" is a corruption of "St. Branwallader") was a Celtic or Welsh monk, who is said to have been a bishop in Jersey, although at the time Jersey would have been part of the ancient diocese of Dol. He has also been said to have been the son of the Cornish king, Kenen. As with many of the early saints of this part of the world, there is little reliable information extant. It is believed that he worked with St. Samson (28th July) in Cornwall and the Channel Islands, where the Parish of St. Brelade in Jersey is dedicated to him, as is the Parish of St. Breward in Cornwall. It is also possible that he travelled with St. Samson to Brittany, where he has sometimes been confused with SS. Brendan (16th May) and Brannoc (7th January).

His feast was kept at Winchester, Exeter, and Cornwall (in Cornwall on 9th February and 6th June — 19th January most likely being the translation of his relics) at least from the tenth century A.D. King Athelstan, founder of Milton Abbey in Dorset, obtained some of the saint's relics (an arm or head), translating them to Milton Abbey in A.D. 935. The full name of Milton Abbey being the *Abbey Church of St. Mary, St. Samson, and St. Branwalader.*

20ᵀᴴ JANUARY

FECHIN — SEVENTH CENTURY

A native of Co. Sligo in Connaught and the founder of several
monasteries in that region; St. Fechin is principally remembered for
founding the monastery at Fore (Fobar), Co. Westmeath. Ecclefechan and
St. Vigean's near Arbroath in Scotland also perpetuate his memory. He is
said to have lived a life of extraordinary penance, spending his nights
reciting the entire Psalter. St. Fechin reposed circa A.D. 665.

MOLAGGA (LAICIN) — SEVENTH CENTURY

Though there are several Saints of the same name (most Irish
hagiographers count at least twelve), and it is often difficult to disentangle
their Lives, it is believed this St. Molagga was a disciple of St. David of
Wales (1ˢᵗ March). Returning to his native Ireland, he founded a
monastery at what is now Fermoy (Irish: *Mainistir Fhear Maí*, meaning
"monastery of the Men of the Plain") Co. Cork. He was distinguished for
his exceptional learning and piety as well as his Christian charity. St.
Molagga seems to have survived the Great Pestilence of A.D. 664, reposing
circa A.D. 655, and is greatly venerated in the South of Ireland.

21ˢᵀ January

Brigid (Briga) — Sixth Century

Known as St. Brigid of Kilbride, in Lismore, she flourished in the late fifth, or early sixth centuries. According to legend, St. Brigid of Kildare (1ˢᵗ February) visited her more than once at Kilbride. According to Colgan*, the now-lost Calendar of Cashel styles her St. Brigid of Killbrige.

Lawdog — Sixth Century

Four churches in the Welsh diocese of St. David's are named for this sixth century A.D. saint. There is no further information about him extant.

Vimin (Wynnin, Gwynnin) — Sixth Century

There being no reliable information on this saint extant, we are left to legend to piece together a Life of sorts. He seems to have been the founder and first Abbot of the monastery of Holywood in Fife, and according to one tradition was a bishop. St. Vimin reposed A.D. 579. Forbes' *Kalendar of Scottish Saints* has some interesting (though of doubtful reliability) details about him, and the *Aberdeen Breviary** gives the Liturgical Office for the Feast of St. Vivian.

WILGILS — SEVENTH CENTURY

Born in Northumbria, he was the father of St. Willibrord (7th November). Withdrawing from the world he built a hermitage dedicated to St. Andrew (30th November) on the banks of the River Humber where he lived as an anchorite.

22ND JANUARY

BRITHWALD — ELEVENTH CENTURY

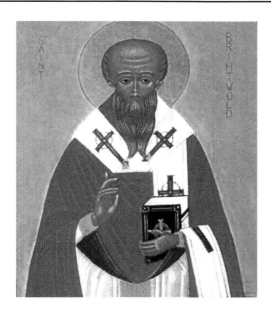

A monk at Glastonbury, St. Brithwald was consecrated Bishop of Ramsbury on the Translation of St. Alfric (16th November) to the See of Canterbury (A.D. 996).   He was known for his gifts of visions and prophecy, and endowed Glastonbury and Malmesbury abbeys.   St. Brithwald reposed A.D. 1043 and was buried at Glastonbury.

23RD JANUARY

COLMAN OF LISMORE — SEVENTH CENTURY

He was Abbot and Bishop of Lismore Co. Waterford.   During St. Colman's tenure as abbot, Lismore grew in fame, attracting a great number of disciples. St. Colman was the spiritual father of numerous holy men and illustrious prelates, and reposed A.D. 702.

Cadoc (Docus, Cathmael, Cadvaci) – Sixth Century

St. Cadoc was a son of Gwynllyw, King of Gwynllwg in South Wales, and Gwladys, the daughter of King Brychan of Brycheiniog, and a nephew of St. Petroc (4ᵗʰ June). He founded the famous monastery of Llancarfan in Glamorgan, which grew to be an illustrious nursery of holy men. Accompanied by St. Gildas (29ᵗʰ January), he assumed an hermetic life on an island off the coast of Vannes in Brittany. After several years, he returned to Britain, settling in the settled in the Eastern counties, and, it is believed, taking spiritual charge of the Britons. St. Cadoc was martyred by the conquering Saxons circa A.D. 580, near Weedon in Northamptonshire.

GUASACHT — FIFTH CENTURY

The son of Maelchu, St. Guasacht was St. Patrick's (17th March) master while St. Patrick was enslaved in Ireland. St. Guasacht was converted by St. Patrick, and eventually became one of his workers in the conversion of the Irish, and ultimately was consecrated Bishop of Granard (Co. Longford).

25TH JANUARY

DWYNWEN — FIFTH CENTURY

A Welsh saint believed to have been a daughter of King of Brychan of Brycheiniog, churches dedicated to her are to be found in Wales and Cornwall. Her holy well and shrine at Llanddwyn in Anglesey were once centres of pilgrimage. After a troubled life, she reposed circa A.D. 460.

EOCHOD (EUCHADIUS) — SIXTH CENTURY

Known as the Apostle to the Scots and Picts in Galloway, St. Eochod was one of St. Columba of Iona's (9th June) twelve companions when he travelled from Ireland to Scotland. There is no reliable information on his life extant; however, it is thought that he was chosen to preach in northern England and Galloway.

SIGEBERT — SEVENTH CENTURY

He was the First Christian King of East Anglia. The principal source for King St. Sigebert is St. Bede the Venerable (25th May), from whom we learn that he was the first English king to receive a Christian baptism and education before his succession, as well as the first to abdicate in order to enter the monastic life. With the help of St. Felix (8th March), the founder of the See of Dunwich, and St. Fursey (16th January), St. Sigebert induced his subjects to embrace Christianity. By the time Penda of Mercia threatened the East Anglians, he had retired into a monastery; but his people recalled Sigebert, and he fell in battle (A.D. 635). As he was fighting against Pagans, he was venerated as a martyr.

THORGYTH (TORTGITH) — SEVENTH CENTURY

The novice-mistress of Barking Abbey under St. Etheldreda of Ely (23ʳᵈ June), and friend of its founder, St. Ethelburga (11ᵗʰ October), she was known for her zeal and care for the young. She was described as a miracle of patience under suffering, as she is reputed to have suffered paralysis for six years and experienced a vision of Ethelburga just before the abbess's death. St. Thorgyth reposed circa A.D. 700.

26TH JANUARY

CONAN — SEVENTH CENTURY

One of the early bishops of the Isle of Man, he was born in Ireland and became a monk at Iona*. While the Bollandists* place St. Conan amongst the early bishops of Man, and Colgan* gives an account of his life and labours, the history of the Isle of Man of this era is quite obscure, and it is almost impossible to state any facts certainty. St. Conan is believed to have reposed circa A.D. 648.

27TH JANUARY

NATALIS (NAILE) — SIXTH CENTURY

St. Natalis was a spiritual child of St. Columba of Iona (9th June), and the founder of monasticism in Ulster. He served as Abbot at St. Naul's, Inver (Co. Donegal), Kinawley (Cill Naile, Co. Fermanagh), Inver Naile (at Raphoe, Co. Donegal) and at Devenish (Daimhinis) Island where he was the successor of St. Laisrén mac Nad Froíc (18th April). His holy well at Kinawley Church is still venerated.

28TH JANUARY

CANNERA (CAINDER, KINNERA) — SIXTH CENTURY

St. Cannera was an Irish holy virgin who, from a young age, lived as an anchoress near Bantry Co. Cork. After receiving a vision of St. Senan's (8th March) sanctity, she sought him out, and, having received Holy Communion at his hands, reposed circa A.D. 530. She was buried at St. Senan's monastery on Scattery Island (Inis Cathaigh).

GLASTIAN (GLASTIANUS, MAC-GLASTIAN) — NINTH CENTURY

St. Glastian was a Scottish bishop who acted as a mediator between the Picts and the Scots during their last civil war. Serving as the comforter, spiritual father, and charitable protector of many thousands of both nations, he did much to alleviate the suffering of the Picts under the subjugation of the Scots. He reposed A.D. 830 and is the patron saint of Kinglassie (Cille MoGhlasaidh) in his native Fife, and is venerated in Kyntire as well.

29ᵀᴴ January

Blath (Flora) — Sixth Century

There are several Saints by the name of Blath (Latinised as Flora) listed in the Irish Martyrologies. While there is little information extant about them, we know of this nun, a humble woman of great sanctity, who fulfilled the obedience of cook at St. Brigid's (1ˢᵗ February) monastery in Kildare. According to the *Martyrology of Donegal* she reposed A.D. 523.

Dallán Forgaill (of Cluain Dallain) — Sixth Century

(Also known as Dallán Forchella; Dallán of Cluain Dalláin; born Eochaid Forchella.) Born in Connaught and a relative of St. Áedan of Ferns (31ˢᵗ January), he was a renowned scholar who went blind from his work (Dallán means "little blind one"). He was the author of a poem in honour of St. Columba of Iona (9ᵗʰ June), called *Ambra Choluim Kille*, published after St. Columba's repose. There is a legend that upon publication of the poem St. Dallán's sight was miraculously restored. He was martyred by pirates at Inis-coel A.D. 598, who threw his severed head into the sea. According to legend, it was recovered and miraculously reunited with his body.

Voloc — Eighth Century

Voloc was a saint in Scotland of possible Irish birth or parentage. Nothing certain is known about this saint, and some authorities believe he

may the same as Fáelchú mac Dorbbéni, who served as Abbot of Iona*
A.D. 713 – 722 (reposing A.D. 724), and who introduced the Roman
tonsure into that Celtic monastery.

30TH JANUARY

TUDY (TUDCLYD, TYBIE, TYDIE) — FIFTH CENTURY

Nothing certain is known about this saint other than she was one of the twenty-four children of Brychan of Brycheiniog. She has left her name to Llandybie in Carmarthenshire in Wales.

31ST JANUARY

ADAMNAN — SEVENTH CENTURY

Not to be confused with Adamnán (Adam, Eunan) of Iona (23rd September), this saint was a native of Ireland who became a monk at Coldingham in present day Scotland. Though there is no reliable information about this saint extant, he seems to have assisted St. Ebba (25th August) in reforming the discipline of the convent which she founded. St. Adamnan reposed circa A.D. 679.

ÁEDAN (AIDAN, MÁEDÓC) — SEVENTH CENTURY

St. Áedan was the founder and first Abbot of a monastery at, and first Bishop of, Ferns, Co. Wexford in Ireland. Born in Co. Cavan to Setna, a tribal chieftain and Eithne, he was also a first cousin of St. Dallán Forgaill (29th January). According to legend when it came time to baptise him there was no boat to take the infant St. Áedan to the mainland, so he is said to have been miraculously floated across the lake on a slab of stone to where St. Kilian (29th July) was waiting to perform the baptism. The holy water font in St. Mogue's Church in Bawnboy is said to be made from part of that stone.

After studies at the great school of St. Finian (12th December) at Clonard, and in Wales, under St. David (1st March), he returned to Ireland (A.D. 580) and was made first Bishop of the newly created See of Ferns.

St. Áedan founded thirty churches and a number of monasteries. The first of these monasteries was on the island of Inis Breachmhaigh where he was born. He also founded monasteries at Drumlane, near Milltown in Co. Cavan, at Ferns in Co. Wexford, in Wales, at Disert-Nairbre in Co. Waterford and finally in Rossinver in Co. Leitrim where, he reposed on the shore of Lough Melvin on 31st January, A.D. 632. He was buried there in the church that he had founded. A bronze reliquary in which his relics were kept is currently preserved in Dublin.

MADOES (MADIANUS) — SEVENTH CENTURY

A saint about whom there is no reliable information extant, aside from being the source of the name for a village in the Carse of Gowrie. According to some authorities he is the same as St. Maedoc (Áedan of Ferns - *vide supra*), whilst others claim him to have been one of St. Boniface Curitan's (14ᵗʰ March) fellow missionaries. However, it is impossible to disentangle the facts from the legends of this holy man.

1ˢᵀ FEBRUARY

BRIGID (BRIDGET, BRIDE) — SIXTH CENTURY

The "Mary of Ireland"; our venerable Mother Brigid of Kildare, or Brigid of Ireland (Bridget, Bride; Gaelic: Naomh Bhríd), was an Irish nun, abbess, and founder of several convents. Along with St. Patrick of Ireland (17ᵗʰ March) and St. Columba of Iona (9ᵗʰ June), she is one of the three patron saints of Ireland.

TROPARION - TONE 1

O holy Brigid, you became sublime through your humility,
and flew on the wings of your longing for God.
When you arrived in the eternal City and appeared before your Divine Spouse,
wearing the crown of virginity,
you kept your promise to remember those who have recourse to you.

You shower grace upon the world, and multiply miracles.
Intercede with Christ our God that He may save our souls.

KONTAKION - TONE 4
The holy virgin Brigid full of divine wisdom,
went with joy along the way of evangelical childhood,
and with the grace of God attained in this way the summit of virtue.
She now bestows blessings upon those who come to her with faith.
O holy Virgin, intercede with Christ our God
that He may have mercy on our souls.

According to tradition, St. Brigid was born at Faughart near Dundalk, Co. Louth, Ireland to Dubhthach, a pagan chieftain of Leinster, and Brocca, a Christian Pictish slave who had been baptized by St. Patrick. Known for her compassion for the poor even as a youth — giving away her family's food and even valuable possessions to those in need — and despite family objections, she was drawn to the monastic life. After her family saw there was no possibility to convince her to pursue a life in the world, a young St. Brigid received monastic tonsure at the hands of St. Mel of Ardagh (6ᵗʰ February). Soon after, she established a monastery on land called Cill Dara (Kildare), or "the church of the oak" which had been given to her by the King of Leinster, thus founding women's coenobitic monasticism in Ireland. Under St. Brigid's leadership this monastery grew to become one of the most prestigious in Ireland, and famous throughout Christian Europe. Renowned for her common-sense and most of all for her holiness, even in her lifetime she was regarded as a saint.

St. Brigid reposed circa A.D. 525 and was buried in a tomb before the high altar of her monastery. During the Danish invasions, her relics were translated to Downpatrick where they were buried with those of St. Patrick of Ireland and St. Columba of Iona. Late in the thirteenth century A.D., her head was extracted and brought to Portugal by three Irish knights on their way to fight in the Holy Land. They left this holy relic in the parish church of Lumiar in northern Lisbon. Portions of the relic were brought back to Ireland in A.D. 1929 and placed in a new church of St. Brigid in Dublin.

CINNIA — FIFTH CENTURY

St. Cinna was a princess of the Kingdom of Ulster, who, upon becoming a Christian, became a nun and entered a monastery under the care of the Abbess Cathuberis. She was responsible for the conversion of many of her Pagan fellow-countrymen and was renowned for miracles. St. Cinna reposed towards the end of the fifth century A.D.

CREWENNA — FIFTH CENTURY

A companion of St. Breaca (4ᵗʰ June) on her trip from Ireland to Cornwall. The only record extant of this saint is the place-name Crowan, near Erth.

DARLUGDACH (DARDULACHA, DERLUGDACH) — SIXTH CENTURY

St. Darlugdach was St. Brigid's (*vide supra*) favourite pupil and her successor as Abbess of Kildare. St. Ultan (4ᵗʰ September), in his *Life of St. Brigit*, writes that at one point Darlugdach had fallen in love, and one evening when she was to have met her lover she left the bed in which she and St. Brigid were sleeping. Knowing the perilousness of what she was about to do, she prayed to God for guidance, placed burning embers in her shoes and then put them on. 'Thus by fire she put out fire, and by pain extinguished pain.' She then returned to bed. St. Brigid, though apparently asleep, knew all, but said nothing. The next day Darlugdach told St. Brigid everything, who then told her she was now safe from the fire of passion here and the fire of hell hereafter; and then St. Brigid healed St. Darlugdach's feet. There is a tradition that St. Brigid told her she would die on the first anniversary of her own repose. St. Darlugdach did in fact repose on the anniversary of St. Brigid's repose circa A.D. 524.

JARLATH (HIERLATH) — FIFTH CENTURY

A disciple of St. Patrick (17th March) and successor of St. Benignus (9th November) to the See of Armagh. Little more is known of him. It appears that St. Jarlath reposed circa A.D. 480.

KINNIA — FIFTH CENTURY

St. Kinna was a holy maiden baptised by St. Patrick (17th March), and then, by him, consecrated to God. She is greatly venerated in Co. Louth.

SEIRIOL — SIXTH CENTURY

This early sixth century A.D. hermit gave his name to the island of Ynys-Seiriol (Puffin Island), off the coast of Anglesey Wales, where the remains of his hermitage still exist. It has been said that he and St. Cybi (8th November) were good friends, and would meet weekly near Llanerchymedd, at the Clorach wells.

2ᴺᴰ February

Feock — Date Uncertain

Aside from a church dedicated to her in Cornwall, her Life is unknown to us. It is possible she was an immigrant from Ireland, and there are some who believe that St. Feock is a variant of Fiacca, a Confessor, friend of St. Patrick, though this is unlikely. Lastly, there are those who identify St. Feock with St. Vouga (15ᵗʰ June) of Brittany.

Laurence of Canterbury — Seventh Century

Second Archbishop of Canterbury he was one of the forty monks sent by Pope St. Gregory the Dialogist with St. Augustine (27ᵗʰ May) to convert the Anglo-Saxons. According to St. Bede the Venerable (25ᵗʰ May), St. Augustine sent St. Laurence back to the Pope to report on the success of converting King Æthelberht of Kent, and to carry a letter with questions for the Pope. He returned with additional monks, as well as Pope St. Gregory the Dialogist's replies to St. Augustine's questions, a document commonly known as the *Libellus responsionum*, that St. Bede the Venerable incorporated in his *Historia ecclesiastica gentis Anglorum**. St. Laurence was consecrated the second Archbishop of Canterbury in A.D. 604, by St. Augustine, in order to assure succession, and guided the young Church skilfully, and successfully, through the crisis that followed the death of King Æthelbert. St. Laurence reposed A.D. 619, and was succeeded by St. Mellitus (24ᵗʰ April).

3RD February

CAELLAINN (CAOILFIONN) — SIXTH CENTURY

She was an Irish saint for whom a church in Roscommon is dedicated. St. Caellainn is thought to have lived in the sixth century A.D.; however, there is no information about her extant.

IA (HIA, IVES) — FIFTH CENTURY

An Irish Princess, and sister of St. Erth (31st October), she travelled to Cornwall with SS. Fingar, Phiala and Companions (14th December). She suffered martyrdom under King Teudar on the River Hayle, A.D. 450. St. Ia has left her name to the Cornish town of St. Ives, which grew up around her grave.

WERBURG (WERBURGH) — SEVENTH CENTURY

The daughter of the Mercian king, Wulfhere, and St. Ermenhild (13th February), St. Werburg (less correctly 'Werburgh'), was placed under the care of her aunt, St. Etheldreda of Ely (23rd June). She lived a life of great sanctity and usefulness eventually becoming abbess, and under the instigation of King Ethelred, worked to reform the monasteries of nuns in his kingdom. St. Werburg also established new monasteries at Trentham and Hanbury (in Staffordshire) and at Weedon (in Northants). She reposed circa A.D. 699 at Trentham, but her relics were translated to Chester (A.D. 875) in the face of Danish invasions. Her shrine, fragments of which are still to be seen in Chester Cathedral, reportedly the site of many miracles, was destroyed during the reign of Henry VIII. St. Werburg is the patron saint of Chester.

WERBURGH — EIGHTH CENTURY

St. Werburgh was a widow who became a nun, most likely at Bardney in England, where she later served as Abbess. It is believed she reposed circa A.D. 785, and nothing further is known about this saint.

4TH FEBRUARY

ALDATE — FIFTH CENTURY?

A Briton who lived in the western counties of England, who in some legends is styled Bishop of Gloucester. Famed for his resistance to heathen invaders, he encouraged his fellow-countrymen to resist as well. This, coupled with his pious and exemplary life, gained him local repute as a saint. There are quite a few West Country churches which bear his name as their titular saint; St. Aldate's in central Oxford also bears his name. It is very possible there were two Saints of this name in fifth or sixth century A.D. England, though reliable details of their lives are lacking; hence, it is all but impossible to disentangle their legends. Notwithstanding this confusion, we may safely place his repose in the middle of the fifth century A.D.

LIEPHARD — SEVENTH CENTURY

A native of England, and possible bishop, according to some legends he was a companion of King Cadwalla in the latter's pilgrimage to Rome. He was martyred near Cambrai in France circa A.D. 640 while on his way back to England. There are those who have confused him with St. Liudhard (24th February), the bishop who attended Queen Bertha to Canterbury; however, neither dates nor ascertained facts support this theory.

MODAN — SIXTH CENTURY

St. Modan was an Irish monk who went to Scotland where he built a chapel at Dryburgh, which grew into the famous Dryburgh Abbey. From this base, he actively preached the Gospel in the Falkirk and Stirling areas, as well as along the Forth. His strict asceticism and great humility lead the community to elect him Abbot of Dryburgh, a position he accepted with great reluctance. After a number of years he resigned and became a hermit in the Dumbarton area, where he lived until his repose. His relics were enshrined at St. Modan's church, Rosneath. In addition, he is the titular saint of the great church at Stirling, and honoured particularly at Dunbarton and Falkirk.

5TH FEBRUARY

INDRACT — EIGHTH CENTURY

Information extant on this saint all dates from several hundred years after his supposed martyrdom, and hence is of questionable reliability. However, it is reasonably certain that he was a descendant of Irish chieftains who lived as a hermit for many years before undertaking a pilgrimage to Rome. While returning from this pilgrimage, he, along with several companions, was murdered by heathens near Glastonbury circa A.D. 710. Their relics were enshrined at Glastonbury Abbey, and they were venerated as martyrs.

6TH FEBRUARY

MEL (MELCHNO) — FIFTH CENTURY

He is commonly believed to have been one of the four sons (Mel, Melchu, Mun, and Rioch) of St. Patrick's (17th March) sister St. Darerca (22nd March) and her husband Conis. They all accompanied their uncle to Ireland with St. Mel becoming the first Bishop of Ardagh. St. Mel reposed circa A.D. 490; he is the patron saint of the Roman Catholic diocese of Ardagh and Clonmacnois, and is commemorated in the name of the cathedral church of the diocese in Longford.

MUN — FIFTH CENTURY

St. Mun was one of the four nephews of St. Patrick (17th March), who joined their uncle in his apostolic labours. St. Patrick consecrated him bishop over the area of the present Co. Longford. St. Mun ended his days as a hermit on an island in Lough Ree.

7ᵀᴴ FEBRUARY

AUGULUS (AUGURIUS, AULE) — FOURTH CENTURY

As with so many saints of his era, there is little in the way of reliable information of his Life extant. The *Martyrology of St. Jerome** lists St. Augulus as a bishop, whilst other ancient authorities describe him as a martyr who laid down his life for Christ in London. This would be in the persecution under Diocletian in which St. Alban (20ᵗʰ June) suffered circa A.D. 303. It is possible St. Augulus was not a saint of the British Isles, as he has also been identified by some French authorities with St. Ouil or Aule of Normandy.

RICHARD — EIGHTH CENTURY

He appears to have been an Anglo-Saxon chieftain or Under-King in Wessex, most likely part of Devonshire. Married to a relative of St. Boniface, the Apostle of Germany, he was the father of three Saints: SS.

Willibald (7th July), Winebald (18th December) and Walburga (25th February). St. Richard reposed at Lucca in Tuscany whilst on a pilgrimage to Rome (A.D. 722). Many miracles, the details of which are now lost to us, testified to his sanctity.

8ᵀᴴ February

Cuthman — Eighth Century

A shepherd, St. Cuthman lived a holy life near Steyning in Sussex, where the old church is dedicated in his honour. Nothing further is known of this saint.

Elfleda (Ælflæd) — Eighth Century

A Saxon princess, she was the daughter of King Oswy of Northumbria. Her father consecrated her to God in infancy, placing her in the care of St. Hilda (17th November) at Whitby. St. Elfleda succeeded St. Hilda as Abbess of Whitby, and was a powerful force in Church affairs. She is said to have mediated a dispute between SS. Wilfrid (12th October) and Theodore of Canterbury (19th September), and to have aided St. Cuthbert (26th October). St. Elfleda reposed A.D. 713.

Kigwe (Kewe, Ciwa) — Date Uncertain

We know nothing certain about this saint. It is likely that she is the same as St. Ciwa, a sixth or seventh century A.D. saint venerated in Monmouthshire. She is listed in the Exeter Martyrology on 8th February, and there is a Welsh Kalendar that lists the name Kigwe or Kigwoe. Alternative spellings include Ciwg and Cwick. It is almost completely certain that she is not the same as St. Keyna (8th October), who has left her name to Keynsham in Somersetshire.

ONCHO (ONCHUO) — SIXTH OR SEVENTH CENTURY

St. Oncho was a pilgrim, a poet, a guardian of sacred traditions, as well as a collector of holy relics in his native Ireland. Whilst on one of his pilgrimages in search of relics, he reposed at Clonmore monastery, which was governed by St. Maidoc (28th February) at that time, and his body was enshrined there, along with the relics he had gathered during his life.

9ᵀᴴ February

CRONAN THE WISE — EIGHTH CENTURY

The little known of this saint leads to the conclusion that he was, in all probability, a Bishop of Lismore, and identical with the holy prelate known there as St. Roman. St. Cronan was best known for his zeal, ability, and success in the regulating of ecclesiastical discipline, and was the author of many sets of disciplinary laws.

CUARAN (CURVINUS, CRONAN) — SEVENTH CENTURY

This Irish saint, who, like many others, was known as "The Wise". St. Curan attempted to conceal his identity and assume the life of a simple monk at Iona*, however, he was eventually recognised by St. Columba (9ᵗʰ June). He most likely reposed well into the eighth century A.D.

EINGAN (EINION, ENEON, ANIANUS) — SIXTH CENTURY

He is believed to have been one of the two sons of the famous chieftain Cunedda, whose family is said to have produced no less than fifty Saints. St. Eingan was a British prince who left Cumberland for Wales, where he finished his days as a hermit at Llanengan near Bangor, reposing circa A.D. 590.

TEIO (TEILIO, TEILUS, THELIAN, TEILAN, TEIOU, TELIOU, DILLO, DILLON) – SIXTH CENTURY

It is difficult to sort through the mass of conflicting traditions concerning this famous saint of South Wales, and compile a reliable account of his life. However, it is fairly certain that he was a disciple of St. Dubritius (14th November), friend of SS. Samson (28th July) and David (1st March), and was the founder of the monastery at Llandeilo Fawr. Records exist of his pilgrimages to Rome and Brittany, where churches bear his name. Legends exist of him having been consecrated bishop at Jerusalem while on a pilgrimage to the Holy Land. He is also said to have succeeded St. Dubricius in the See of Llandaff. St. Teio reposed at Llandeilo Fawr, A.D. 560.

10ᵀᴴ FEBRUARY

MEREWENNA — TENTH CENTURY

Of noble Irish birth, she was the first Abbess of Romsey in Hampshire after its restoration under King Edward the Peaceful. Under her leadership, the monastery prospered and even attracted royalty, including the princess St. Elfleda (8ᵗʰ February). St. Merewenna reposed circa A.D. 970.

TRUMWIN — EIGHTH CENTURY

Consecrated by St. Theodore of Canterbury (19ᵗʰ September) as Bishop of the Southern Picts in Scotland, St. Trumwin was a close friend of St. Cuthbert (26ᵗʰ October). According to St. Bede the Venerable (25ᵗʰ May), he was in attendance at the Synod on the Alne (A.D. 684). He suffered greatly in his work amongst the Picts, and often had to flee from province to province. When the Picts overran his monastery, St. Trumwin retired to Whitby, where he served as spiritual father to the nuns there under St. Elfleda (8ᵗʰ February), reposing in the beginning of the eighth century A.D.

11ᵀᴴ FEBRUARY

CÆDMON — SEVENTH CENTURY

A Northumbrian, who is author of the first recorded poem in English, he is known as the *Father of English Poetry*.

The only source of original information about St. Cædmon is from St. Bede the Venerable's (25th May) *Historia ecclesiastica**, in which he relates that St. Cædmon was a lay brother who worked and cared for the animals at Whitby Abbey. One evening, while the monks were feasting, singing, and playing a harp, St. Cædmon left early to sleep with the animals because he knew no songs. St. Bede the Venerable (25th May) implies that St. Cædmon felt he lacked the knowledge needed to compose the words to songs. While sleeping, Cædmon had a dream in which "someone" (*quidam*) approached him and asked him to sing *principium creaturarum*, "the beginning of created things". After first refusing to sing, Cædmon subsequently produced a short eulogistic poem praising God, the Creator of heaven and earth.

Upon awakening the next morning, Cædmon not only remembered everything he had sung in his dream, but added additional lines to his poem. After telling his foreman about this dream, he was taken immediately to see the abbess, believed to be St. Hilda (17th November), who closely questioned St. Cædmon about his dream. Satisfied that it was a gift from God, the abbess gave him a new commission as a test; this time for a poem based on "a passage of sacred history or doctrine". Upon returning the next morning with the requested poem, St. Cædmon was ordered to take monastic vows. The abbess then ordered her scholars to teach St. Cædmon sacred history and doctrine, which after a night of reflection; St. Cædmon would turn into the most beautiful poetry. According to St. Bede the Venerable, St. Cædmon was responsible for a great number of splendid vernacular poetic texts on a variety of Christian topics.

After a long and zealously pious life, St. Cædmon, having received a premonition of death, asked to be moved to the abbey's hospice where, having gathered his friends around him, he expired, after receiving the Holy Eucharist circa A.D. 680.

CÆDMON'S HYMN OF CREATION

Nu scylun hergan hefaenricaes uard	Now we should praise the heaven-kingdom's guardian,
metudæs maecti end his modgidanc	the measurer's might and his mind-conception,
uerc uuldurfadur sue he uundra gihuaes	work of the glorious father, as we each wonder,
eci dryctin or astelidæ	eternal Lord, instilled at the origin.
he aerist scop aelda barnum	He first created for men's sons
heben til hrofe haleg scepen	heaven as a roof, holy creator;
tha middungeard moncynnæs uard	then, middle-earth, mankind's guardian,
eci dryctin æfter tiadæ	eternal Lord, afterward made
firum foldu frea allmectig	the earth for men, father almighty.

GOBNATA (GOBNET) – SIXTH CENTURY

According to legend, an angel appeared to St. Gobnata one day and told her to leave her home, and to keep walking until she found nine white deer. She saw three white deer at Clondrohid, Co. Cork, and decided to follow them. Then, at Ballymakeera, she saw six white deer. Finally, at Ballyvourney she came upon nine white deer grazing in a wood. There she was given land for a women's monastery by her spiritual father, St. Abban of Kill-Abban, Co. Laois (16ᵗʰ March), and he installed her as abbess. A holy well still exists there named for St. Gobnata. The patron saint of Ballyvourney, she is venerated throughout southern Ireland; there are churches dedicated to her in Waterford and Kerry. She is also revered in Scotland. The exact year of her repose is unknown, though it was most probably in the sixth century A.D.

TROPARION – (TONE 3):

As a spiritual child of the God-inspired Abban,
Thou didst worthily guide many into monastic virtue,
most holy Gobnata
Wherefore we entreat thee to intercede for us that we
may be guided aright and be found worthy of the great
mercy of Christ our God.

KONTAKION – (TONE 5):

Praise and honour are thy due
O physician of bodies and souls,
Most Pious Gobnata.
As thou, being blessed with the gift of healing,
Didst bring to many the wholeness and peace of Christ,
Pray now for us that our tormented souls
May come to know the joy of godly healing.

12ᵀᴴ FEBRUARY

ETHILWOLD — EIGHTH CENTURY

A disciple of St. Cuthbert (20th March), St. Ethilwold went on to serve as Abbot of Melrose in Scotland. For the last twenty years of his life, he was Bishop of Lindisfarne. He was a contemporary of St. Bede the Venerable (25th May), who spoke of him with great praise. St. Ethelwold reposed A.D. 750, and was initially buried at Lindisfarne, though his relics were later translated to Durham.

13ᵀᴴ February

Dyfnog — Seventh Century

A Welsh saint of the family of Caradog, he was greatly venerated in Clwyd. No further information on this saint is extant.

Ermenhild (Ermengild, Ermenilda) — Seventh Century

St. Ermenhild was the daughter of King Erconbert of Kent and St. Saxburgh (6th July), as well as the wife of King Wulfhere of Mercia, and the mother of St. Werburgh (3rd February). Upon the death of her husband, she joined her mother at the Abbey of Minster in Sheppey, and eventually succeeded her as abbess. She later joined her daughter St. Etheldreda's (23rd June) monastery at Ely, where they remained for the rest of their earthly lives. It is thought the repose of St. Ermenild may have taken place about A.D. 700.

Huna — Seventh Century

St. Huna was a priest-monk at Ely under St. Audrey (Etheldred) (23rd June), to whom he attended during the last moments of her life. He subsequently became a hermit in the fens near Chatteris, at a place now called Honey Farm after him, reposing circa A.D. 690.

MODOMNOCK (DOMNOC, DOMINIC) — SIXTH CENTURY

An Irish saint, perhaps of the O'Neil Clan, he was a disciple of St. David (1st March) in Wales. He returned to Ireland where he lived as a hermit near Kilkenny. According to legend, St. Modomnock introduced bees to Ireland when a swarm followed him from his monastery in Wales where he had been a beekeeper. St. Modomnock reposed circa A.D. 550.

14TH FEBRUARY

CONRAN — DATE UNKNOWN

Little is known about St. Conran, other than that he was a Bishop of the Orkney Islands, known for his austere life and zealousness in pastoring souls. In the past he was held in great veneration in the North of Scotland.

15TH FEBRUARY

BERACH (BARACHIAS, BERACHIUS) — SIXTH CENTURY

A disciple of St. Kevin (3rd June), St. Berach founded a monastery at Clusin-Coirpte (now Termonbarry from the Irish: *Tearmann Bearaigh*, meaning "St. Barry's sanctuary") in Connaught. He is venerated in Co. Roscommon and is the patron saint of Kilbarry near Dublin.

DOCHOW (DOCHAU, DOGWYN) — DATE UNCERTAIN

There is a fair degree of uncertainty surrounding this saint. He is mentioned in the *English Menology* as a Welsh saint, though he may be the same as St. Cadoc (24th January), sometimes called St. Dockoe, or St. Dogmæl, St. Docmæl. There is a church in north-east Wales dedicated to a St. Docwy, or Dogway. It is probable that he was the founder of a monastery in Cornwall, and the *Annals of Ulster* describes him as a bishop.

FARANNAN — SIXTH CENTURY

A native of Ireland St. Farannan went to Iona* to become a disciple of St. Columba (9th June). He later settled in the West of Ireland, where he lived as an anchorite in a cave in the strictest asceticism, reposing circa A.D. 590. He is the patron saint of Alterna (All-Faranna) in Sligo, the probable place of his death.

16TH FEBRUARY

There are no Saints of the British Isles listed on the Calendar for this date.

17ᵀᴴ February

Finan — Seventh Century

An Irishman by birth, he succeeded St. Aidan (31ˢᵗ August) as Bishop of Lindisfarne. In his earlier life as a monk at Iona*, St. Finan was a strong supporter of the Celtic ecclesiastical traditions, opposing the successors of St. Augustine of Canterbury (27ᵗʰ May), who strove to bring English customs into closer conformity with those of Rome. He converted Kings Peada of Mercia and Sigebert of Essex to Christianity, and along with St. Cedd and others, evangelised the most southern regions of England. St. Finan reposed A.D. 661.

FINTAN — SIXTH CENTURY

St. Fintan lived as an anchorite at Clonenagh in Leinster. In time numerous disciples, including St. Comgall of Bangor (10ᵗʰ May), and St. Columba (12ᵗʰ December) gathered around St. Fintan who became their abbot. He has been compared by the Irish annalists to St. Benedict, and is styled *"Father of the Irish Monks"*. St. Fintan reposed A.D. 603.

FORTCHERN — FIFTH CENTURY

He was the son of a chieftain of Trim, and one of St. Patrick's (17ᵗʰ March) earliest converts in Ireland. St. Fortchern devoted himself to the service of St. Patrick, and is said to have refused to be consecrated bishop out of humility. Unfortunately, the details of his life have been intertwined with that of St. Loman (*vide infra*), hence nothing further about this saint can be said with any degree of certainty.

LOMAN (LUMAN) — FIFTH CENTURY

The first Bishop of Trim in Meath, St. Loman is said to have been a nephew of St. Patrick (17ᵗʰ March). He seems to have reposed in the mid-fifth century A.D. Unfortunately, the details of his life have been intertwined with that of St. Fortchern (*vide supra*), hence nothing further about this saint can be said with any degree of certainty.

18ᵀᴴ FEBRUARY

COLMAN OF LINDISFARNE — SEVENTH CENTURY

Our father among the saints Colman of Lindisfarne was a monk of the seventh century Church of Scotland and Ireland. He led the Celtic party at the Synod of Whitby*. His defence of the Celtic rite led to his identification as the Last of the Columban Abbots of Lindisfarne.

Born in Connaught, Ireland little is known of his early life. St. Colman was tonsured a monk at Iona*, was a disciple of St. Columba (9ᵗʰ June) and a contemporary of SS. Finian (16ᵗʰ March) and Aidan (31ˢᵗ August). Following the repose of St. Finian, Colman was chosen to succeed him as the third Abbot/Bishop of Lindisfarne. Noted for his austere and zealous life, and held in high repute for his sanctity, his episcopate was an exemplar of frugality and simplicity of living, as well as the devotion of his clergy to their responsibilities of preaching and ministering to the faithful. St. Colman's defence of Celtic tradition and reluctance to yield to the Roman rite fixing the date of Easter (see *Paschal Controversy**) led to the Synod of Whitby*. Though he put forth an eloquent defence, King Oswy made a royal decision to follow the Roman practices. This was a decision that was met with general acceptance, but one, which St. Colman could not accept, resigning from his See. St. Colman left for Iona* with all of the Irish and thirty English monks from Lindisfarne. He remained in Scotland for about three years, establishing several churches, and then returned to his native Ireland with about thirty Irish and English monks. They settled on the island of Inishbofin in Co. Galway where St. Colman established a monastery and school. In time, friction developed between the Irish and English monks; St. Colman resolved this by taking the English monks to the Irish mainland, where he established a monastery which he called Mayo of the Saxons, which went on to become an important centre of sanctity and learning, and in time an Episcopal See. St. Colman returned to Inishbofin, where he reposed A.D. 675.

ETHELINA (EUDELME) — DATE UNKNOWN

St. Ethelina is the patron saint of Little Sodbury in present-day Gloucestershire. No further information, including the dates of her life, is extant.

19TH FEBRUARY

ODRAN — FIFTH CENTURY

Whilst he is traditionally believed to have been St. Patrick's (17th March) charioteer and the first Irish martyr circa A.D. 452, there is no reliable information on this saint extant.

20ᵀᴴ February

Bolcan (Olcan) — Fifth Century

St. Bolcan was baptised by St. Patrick (17ᵗʰ March), who sent him to study in Gaul. After his return to Ireland, St. Patrick consecrated him Bishop of Derkan (which was most likely near Armoy) in Ulster. St. Bolcan also founded a school in his See, which was one of the most eminent of its day. He reposed circa A.D. 480.

Colgan — Eighth Century

A renowned Abbot of Clonmacnoise, and one of the many of his era called 'the Wise', St. Colgan was also called 'the Chief Scribe of the Irish'. He was a friend of Alcuin, and venerated even during his lifetime. Some of the prayers he composed are still extant. St. Colgan reposed circa A.D. 796.

21ˢᵗ FEBRUARY

There are no Saints of the British Isles listed on the Calendar for this date.

22ᴺᴰ February

Elwin — Sixth Century

Though no reliable Life is extant, it seems that St. Elwin accompanied St. Breaca (4ᵗʰ June) and six others from Ireland to Cornwall in the sixth century A.D. A chapel in Sithney parish, Cornwall, has been dedicated to St. Elwen since the 13ᵗʰ century A.D., and in Brittany, several sites and place names are associated with possibly related figures.

John the Saxon — Ninth Century

A native of Friesland who was invited to England by King Alfred, along with other holy and learned men, to restore monasticism in England following the Danish invasions . He was made Abbot of Athelney in Somersetshire, where his zeal for the restoration of Religious discipline led to his being murdered whilst kneeling in prayer in his oratory, A.D. 985.

23RD FEBRUARY

BOSWELL (BOISIL) — SEVENTH CENTURY

St. Boswell served as a Prior of Melrose Abbey, and later successor of Abbot St. Eata (26th October). According to St. Bede the Venerable (25th May) he was a man of great virtue who also had the gift of prophecy, foretelling the Great Pestilence of A.D. 664 three years in advance. His disciples included SS. Cuthbert (20th March) and Egbert (24th April), both of whom greatly admired him, as did St. Bede the Venerable (25th May). St. Boswell reposed during the plague he had foretold, A.D. 664.

MILBURGH (MILBURGA OR MILDBURH) — EIGHTH CENTURY

A daughter of Merewalh, sub-king of the Magonsæte, a western cadet kingdom of Mercia, and St. Ermenburga (19th November), St. Milburgh was also the sister of SS. Mildred of Minster-in-Thanet (13th July) and Mildgytha (17th January). She was the second Abbess of Wenlock, a wonder-worker, was said to have healed the blind and lepers, and was known for power over birds as well. St. Milburgh reposed A.D. 715.

24ᵀᴴ February

Cumine the White — Seventh Century

An Irishman who served as Abbot of Iona*, St. Cumine also wrote a Life of St. Columba of Iona (9ᵗʰ June). He reposed A.D. 669.

Liudhard (Letard) — Sixth Century

St. Liudhard was the French bishop of unknown See - though Butler*, and some others assert that he had been Bishop of Senlis in Picardy, who accompanied Queen Bertha to Kent on the occasion of her marriage to King St. Ethelbert (25ᵗʰ February). As with so many of his contemporaries, few definite facts are known of his life, though it is safe to assume he did have a role in ensuring the warm welcome given to St. Augustine (27ᵗʰ May) and his fellow missionaries. St. Liudhard reposed circa A.D. 600.

25TH FEBRUARY

ETHELBERT (ALBERT) OF KENT — SEVENTH CENTURY

The first English Christian king, St. Ethelbert was married to Bertha of France . He welcomed the mission led by St. Augustine (27th May) in A.D. 597, and is believed to have been baptised by him that same year. He founded Canterbury and Rochester Cathedrals, as well as St. Paul's, London. He reposed A.D. 616, and was buried in the abbey, which he had also built at Canterbury.

26TH FEBRUARY

There are no Saints of the British Isles listed on the Calendar for this date.

27TH FEBRUARY

ALNOTH — SEVENTH CENTURY

The bailiff at St. Werburgh's (3rd February) monastery at Weedon in Northamptonshire, St. Alnoth later lived as an anchorite at Stowe. He was martyred there by bandits circa A.D. 700.

COMGAN — SIXTH CENTURY

St. Comgan was an Abbot of Glenthsen or Killeshin in Ireland who reposed circa A.D. 565. Nothing further is known of this saint.

HEREFRITH — NINTH CENTURY

A Bishop of Lindsey, St. Herefrith was most likely martyred by the Danes circa A.D. 869. It is entirely possible that he was the last Bishop of Lindsey before the Danes wintered at Torksey in A.D. 872-3, after which the episcopal succession ceased. His relics were amongst those translated by St. Ethelwold (1st August) to Thorney. There was a church of St. Herefrith at Louth mentioned in several records from the 13th – 15th centuries A.D.

28TH FEBRUARY

LLIBIO — SIXTH CENTURY

St. Llibio is the patron saint of Llanlibio in the Isle of Anglesea. According to Baring-Gould* he was one of the sons of Seithenin, who, along with his brothers, joined Dwnawd's monastery at Bangor after the flooding of the Plain of Gwyddno.

MAIDOC (MADOC) — SIXTH CENTURY

There is no definitive information on this saint extent, though it is most likely he is the sixth century A.D. bishop (or perhaps only abbot), after whom Llanmadog in Glamorganshire is called.

OSWALD — TENTH CENTURY

Born in England to Danish nobles, St. Oswald was the nephew of St. Oda of Canterbury (2nd June) under whom he began his studies. He later went to Fleury to continue his studies and receive monastic tonsure, and was later ordained to the priesthood. Returning to England, St. Oswald was consecrated Bishop of Worcester, and worked with SS. Dunstan (19th May) and Ethelwold (1st August), with great success, to revive monastic life, and religious discipline in Anglo-Saxon England. He personally founded monasteries at Ramsey and at Worcester, and was subsequently promoted to the Archbishopric of York (A.D. 972). St. Oswald reposed whilst on his knees engaged in his daily practice of washing the feet of twelve poor people, circa A.D. 990.

SILLAN (SILVANUS) — SEVENTH CENTURY

A disciple of St. Comgall (10th May) at Bangor in Co. Down, and one of his successors there as abbot. Although there is no further certain knowledge of him, he seems to have had a great reputation for sanctity. Various sources have placed the year of his repose as A.D. 606 and A.D. 610.

1ˢᵀ MARCH

DAVID — SEVENTH CENTURY

Our father among the saints David of Wales, known in Welsh as Dewi Sant, is the patron saint of Wales and considered by many to be one of the most illustrious of the ancient British bishops. He is also known as the Dewi Ddyfrwr (David the Water Drinker) due to his habit of drinking only water and the creation of many holy wells associated with his life.

Though there is no reliable Life extant, legend has it that St. David was born to noble parents in South Wales and educated by St. Paulinus (23ʳᵈ November), the disciple of St. Germanus of Auxerre (31ˢᵗ July). He was a staunch opponent of the Pelagian* heresy, and the founder of the See of St. David's or Menevia. To which, when appointed to succeed St.

Dubricius (14th November), he transferred the primary Welsh Bishopric from Caerleon. The foundation of a dozen monasteries and many miracles are attributed to St. David, and he is said to have been zealous in encouraging discipline among both clergy and laity, and to have presided over the Synod of Brefi circa A.D. 560. The date of his repose is listed as anywhere from the mid-sixth century A.D. to circa A.D. 601. His relics survive and are enshrined in St. David's Cathedral, St. Davids, Pembrokeshire.

MARNOCK (MARNANUS, MARNAN, MARNOC) – SEVENTH CENTURY

A native of Ireland, St. Marnock spent time at Iona* with St. Columba (9th June), and later served as a bishop, though the name of the See is lost to time. He reposed in Annandale in Scotland circa A.D. 625, and was much venerated on the Scottish border. Kilmarnock in Scotland is named for him.

MONAN – NINTH CENTURY

St. Monan began as a disciple of St. Adrian (4th March) at St. Andrews in Scotland, and later was a missionary along the Firth of Forth. Along with six thousand other Christians, he was slain by the Danes (A.D. 874). His relics were held in great veneration at Innerny (present-day St. Monans) in Fife, the place of his martyrdom, and were famous for miracles.

2ᴺᴰ March

Chad (Ceadda) – Seventh Century

St. Chad was a native of Northumbria, brother of St. Cedd of London (26ᵗʰ October), pupil of St. Aidan at Lindisfarne, and later studied in Ireland. On his return to England he was made Abbot of Lastingham, where he became known for his ability as a pastor and holiness of life. During St. Wilfrid's (12ᵗʰ October) absence in France, St. Chad was irregularly consecrated Bishop of the Northumbrians, with his See at York in St. Wilfrid's place. However upon St. Wilfrid's return, Archbishop St. Theodore of Canterbury (19ᵗʰ September) denied the legitimacy of St. Chad's consecration, and, with great humility, St. Chad accepted this decision and retired to Lastingham. Impressed by his action, St. Theodore regularized his consecration and made him Bishop of Lichfield. St. Chad was a tireless evangelist and journeyed as far as north Lincolnshire in spreading the Gospel, and is said to have founded the monastery at Barrow. St. Chad reposed A.D. 673 during the great pestilence, leaving behind a reputation for zeal and devotion. He was buried at the Cathedral in Birmingham, where his relics are preserved to this day.

CYNIBIL (CYNIBILD) – SEVENTH CENTURY

A brother of SS. Chad (*vide supra*), and Cedd (26ᵗʰ October), and of Caelin, all of whom worked to enlighten England. Amongst their works was the founding of the monastery at Lastingham. St. Bede the Venerable (25ᵗʰ May) comments on how unusual it was for four brothers to all enter the priesthood, two of them becoming bishops. The exact year of St. Cynibil's repose in the seventh century A.D. is unknown.

FERGNA – SEVENTH CENTURY

Called 'the White', he was a relative, disciple, and successor of St. Columba (9ᵗʰ June) as Abbot of Iona. St. Fergna reposed, as Abbot of Iona, A.D. 637.

GISTILIAN (GISTLIAN) – SIXTH CENTURY

St. Gistilian was the uncle of St. David of Wales (1ˢᵗ March), as well as a monk at St. David's - Menevia. There is no further information on this saint extant.

SLEBHENE (SLEBHINE) — EIGHTH CENTURY

An Irishman who was a monk at Iona, St. Slebhene served as its fifteenth abbot from A.D. 752 until his repose A.D. 767.

3RD MARCH

CELE-CHRIST — EIGHTH CENTURY

St. Cele-Christ (Worshipper of Christ) led an hermetic life for many years, before being forced to accept a bishopric in Leinster. According to *The Annals of Ulster*, he reposed A.D. 728. There is no further information on his life extant.

FOILA (FAILE, FOILENNA, FALLENA) — SIXTH CENTURY

Believed to have been the sister of St. Colgan (20th February), together they are the patrons of the parishes of Kil-Faile (Kileely) and Kil-Colgan, in Co. Galway. Kil-faile has been a noted place of pilgrimage. A written record of her life called *The Acts of St. Foila* is no longer extant.

LAMALISSE — SEVENTH CENTURY

St. Lamalisse was a Scottish hermit for whom Lamlash on the Isle of Arran is named. No further information on this saint is extant.

NON (NONNA, NONNITA) — SIXTH CENTURY

The mother of St. David of Wales (1st March). St. Non spent her later years in a monastery. She came to be renowned for such sanctity that, following her repose, churches were dedicated to her, including a chapel and well near her son's cathedral at St. David's in Pembrokeshire, and another in Altarnun, on the north-eastern edge of Bodmin Moor, in Cornwall. Though her relics were kept in Cornwall, some claim that she ended her days in Brittany. However, there is insufficient evidence to support this theory. The exact year of St. Non's repose is unknown, though it must have been in the first half of the sixth century A.D.

WINWALOE — SIXTH CENTURY

Born in Brittany to English exiles, St. Winwaloe was related to SS. Cadfan (1st November), Selyf (25th June), and Cybi (8th November). He became a disciple of St. Budoc (9th December) on the Île Lavret. He went on to found the monastery at Landévennec, which he governed until his repose in the first quarter of the sixth century A.D. There are several churches in Cornwall dedicated to him, indicating a connexion between him and that area. Unfortunately there is no reliable Life known to us, and it is difficult to attempt to construct one from various traditions, many of which are contradictory. It is even possible that there may have been more than one saint of his name.

4ᵀᴴ March

Adrian and Companions — Ninth Century

St. Adrian was a bishop (perhaps of St. Andrews) on the Isle of May in the Firth of Forth in Scotland, who along with a group of martyrs (which some sources number in the thousands) who was massacred by the Danes (A.D. 874). There is no further reliable information on this saint's life available to us.

Owen — Seventh Century

A monk who accompanied St. Chad (2ⁿᵈ March) on his mission to the Mercians, St. Owen then served him at Lichfield. Though no Life is extant, tradition has it that he led a most holy life, and by God's Grace, had many heavenly visions. He reposed circa A.D. 680.

5ᵀᴴ March

Caron — Date Unknown

Aside from the fact that he is the patron saint of Tregaron in Dyfed Wales, there is nothing known about this saint.

Carthage the Elder — Sixth Century

St. Carthage the Elder succeeded of St. Kieran (*vide infra*) as Bishop of Ossory in Ireland. He is mainly known as the tutor and foster-father of his namesake, St. Carthage the Younger (14ᵗʰ May). Beyond that, there is no reliable Life of this saint, but he is said by many to have been a son or grandson of King Ængus. He is generally believed to have reposed circa A.D. 540.

Colman of Armagh — Fifth Century

A disciple of St. Patrick (17ᵗʰ March) St. Colman of Armagh was renowned for his extreme asceticism. He predeceased his holy master, who buried him at Armagh.

Kieran (Kieman, Kyran, Ciaran) — Fifth Century

"The First-Born of the Saints of Ireland", St. Kieran was born in Ossory to a noble family. He was most likely consecrated first bishop of Ossory by St.

Patrick (17ᵗʰ March), though there are those who say he was consecrated by the Pope of the time. Regarded as one of the Twelve Apostles of Ireland, he was associated with St. Patrick's work in that land, and was also the founder of a monastery at Saighir. Some claim that he crossed over to Cornwall, and was the same saints as St. Piran (*vide infra*) who is venerated there as a local saint, though this is highly unlikely. St. Kieran reposed circa A.D. 530 at what would have been a very advanced age.

PIRAN (PYRAN) — FIFTH CENTURY

St. Piran was a hermit near Padstow in Cornwall. Like many of his contemporaries, there are many legends but little reliable facts about his life. Often stories of his life have been entangled with that of St. Kieran of Ossory (*vide supra*), and there are some who have argued that he is the same saint as St. Kieran of Clonmacnoise (9ᵗʰ September). St. Piran is venerated as the patron saint of miners, and the town of Perranporth is named after him. He reposed circa A.D. 480.

6TH MARCH

BALDRED (BALTHER) — SEVENTH CENTURY

A Scottish bishop thought by many to have been the successor of St. Kentigern Mungo (13th January) at Glasgow, St. Baldred ended his life as an anchorite at Bass Rock on the coast of the Firth of Forth. He reposed circa A.D. 756 and his relics were enshrined in Durham with those of St. Bilfrid (*vide infra*).

BILFRID (BILLFRITH) — EIGHTH CENTURY

A hermit at Lindisfarne, St. Bilfrid was an expert goldsmith and bound in gold the Lindisfarne Gospels, written and illuminated by St. Edfrith (4th June). His repose took place between A.D. 740 and A.D. 756, though the day is uncertain; 6th March is the anniversary of the translation of his relics, along with those of St. Balther (*vide supra*), to Durham.

CYNEBURGH, CYNESWITH AND TIBBA — SEVENTH CENTURY

SS. Cyneburgh and Cyneswith were daughters of Penda of Mercia in England, who was notorious for his opposition to Orthodoxy. On the death of her husband, Alchfrid of Northumberland, St. Cyneburgh founded a monastery in Castor in Northamptonshire. She was joined by her sister St. Cyneswith, who succeeded her as abbess, and their relative St. Tibba. Circa A.D. 680 is given as the year of their repose, and the relics of all three were enshrined in Peterborough Abbey.

7ᵀᴴ MARCH

DEIFER — SIXTH CENTURY

A Welsh saint, he was the founder and Abbot of Bodfari in Denbighshire. No further information on this saint is extant.

ENODOCH (WENEDOC) — SIXTH CENTURY

St. Enodoch was a Welsh saint and a member of the great Brychan of Brycheiniog family. It is possible she is the same saints as St. Gwen (18th October), daughter of the famous chieftain Brychan of Brycheiniog. Though the exact year of her repose is unknown, it would have been no later than A.D. 520.

EOSTERWINE — SEVENTH CENTURY

A Northumbrian noble and cousin of St. Benedict Biscop (12th January), he entered the monastery of Wearmouth under his cousin at the age of 24. St. Eosterwine was known for his humility and gentleness, refined through a life of constant prayer, as well as for his zeal and skill when serving as abbot in his cousin's absence. St. Eosterwine reposed A.D. 688 and his relics were enshrined with those of St. Benedict Biscop and of St. Sigfrid (22nd August), his successor, before the altar of St. Peter at Wearmouth.

8ᵀᴴ MARCH

BEOADH (BEATUS) — SIXTH CENTURY

A Bishop of Ardcarne in Co. Roscommon, little facts are known of St. Beoadh life. Traditionally he has been renowned for his piety and the miracles that are associated with him. It is believed that he reposed sometime between A.D. 518 and A.D. 523.

FELIX OF DUNWICH — SEVENTH CENTURY

THE APOSTLE OF EAST ANGLIA

TROPARION - TONE 8

Felix of Burgundy, hierarch and teacher, preaching the Word of life,
You did gather a rich harvest of believers;

Together with Furzey of Ireland, pilgrim for the love of the Lord,
Outstanding in virtue, renowned in word and deed;
Enlighteners of East Anglia, we rightly praise you, holy and God-bearing fathers.

KONTAKION - TONE 2

Having come to the land of Sigebert, the righteous king,
You preached the kingdom of Christ our God,
And as a first-fruit the king himself received the tonsure,
Seeking an everlasting kingdom;
And mindful of his monastic vow,
He lay down his life, unarmed in the midst of battle;
Wherefore, O Felix and Furzey, we venerate your memory crying out:
Glory to Christ our King the Redeemer of the World!

A native of Burgundy, who, after converting the then-exiled East Anglian prince, King St. Sigebert (25th January), made his way to England. Establishing his See at Dunwich in Suffolk, St. Felix laboured there for seventeen years, successfully preaching the Gospel to the heathen in East Anglia. He founded a school for boys with the help of King St. Sigebert, which he staffed with teachers from Canterbury. St. Felix reposed A.D. 648, and was buried at Dunwich; his relics were translated to Ramsey in A.D. 971. St. Felix has given his name to Felixstowe in Suffolk, and to Felixkirk in Yorkshire.

RHIAN (RANUS, RIAN) — DATE UNKNOWN

The saint for whom Llanrian in Pembrokeshire is named. He has been described as an abbot by William of Worcester and Leland. Neither specific dates nor particulars facts concerning his life are ascertainable.

Sᴇɴᴀɴ (Sᴇɴᴀᴍᴇs) — Sɪxᴛʜ Cᴇɴᴛᴜʀʏ

St. Senan was a disciple of Abbots Cassidus and Natalis. After establishing a monastery on the Island of Inniscorthy (Leinster) he visited Rome and Gaul, and on his return spent time with St. David (1ˢᵗ March) in Wales. Returning to Ireland, he founded more churches and monasteries, notably one in Iniscarra near Cork, finally settling on Scattery Island in the Shannon estuary, reposing circa A.D. 540.

9ᵀᴴ March

Bosa – Eighth Century

A monk at Whitby, St. Bosa was consecrated Bishop of York by St. Theodore of Canterbury (19th September) during the exile of St. Wilfrid 12th October). St. Bede the Venerable (25th May) recalls St. Bosa as 'A man beloved of God...of most unusual merit and holiness'. St. Bosa reposed A.D. 705.

Constantine – Sixth Century

St. Constantine is described as a Cornish prince who abdicated in favour of his son after the death of his wife. Said to have been "immersed in worldly cares and defiled by vices" prior to his conversion, he repented and is said to have either entered St. David's (1st March) monastery, and then to have been sent as a missionary to the Scots, or to have gone directly to the north, where he worked in the area of the Kintyre Peninsula (formerly Cantyre) in southwest Scotland, founding a monastery at Govan on the Clyde. He was martyred by bandits in Scotland circa A.D. 576.

Whether he was the same Constantine excoriated by St. Gildas the Wise (29th January) in his *De Excidio et Conquestu Britanniæ* * as "...the tyrannical whelp of the unclean lioness of Damnonia," or another prince of the same name, is an open question.

10TH MARCH

FAILBHE THE LITTLE — EIGHTH CENTURY

Abbot of Iona for seven years, he reposed A.D. 754 at the age of eighty. No further information on this saint is extant.

KESSOG (MACKESSOG) — SIXTH CENTURY

St. Kessog is said to have been an Irish prince from Cashel in Tipperary who, even as a child, is said to have worked miracles. St. Kessog left Ireland and became a missionary bishop in Scotland, where he evangelised the Lennox and Southern Perthshire areas until he was martyred (circa A.D. 560). According to one legend, his martyrdom took place at Bandry, where a heap of stones was known as St. Kessog's Cairn.

SEDNA — SIXTH CENTURY

St. Sedna was a Bishop of Ossory and Abbot of Seir-Kieran Abbey, both in Ireland. He reposed circa A.D. 570. There is no further information on his life extant.

SILVESTER — FIFTH CENTURY

A companion of St. Palladius (7th July) in his mission to Ireland. St. Silvester is believed to have reposed circa A.D. 420. No further information on this saint is extant.

11ᵀᴴ March

ÆNGUS (ANGUS) – NINTH CENTURY

Known as 'the Culdee', he was an Irish saint, Abbot at Clonenagh, and then at Tallacht. He later returned to Clonenagh to serve as bishop. He is remembered for his *Félire Óengusso* (*Martyrology of Ængus*), consisting of 365 quatrains, one for each day of the year, framed between a lengthy prologue and epilogue, and is the earliest metrical martyrology to have been written in the vernacular. St. Ængus reposed circa A.D. 830.

12ᵀᴴ MARCH

ALPHEGE THE ELDER — TENTH CENTURY

He was called the Elder to distinguish him from his more famous namesake, the Martyr of Canterbury and Greenwich (19ᵗʰ April). He was a monk of singularly holy life, and encouraged many others to become monks, notably his relative St. Dunstan (19ᵗʰ May), whom he ordained priest. St. Alphege succeeded St. Birnstan 4ᵗʰ November) in the See of Winchester (A.D. 935), where he reposed; his relics were enshrined there (A.D. 951).

MURA MCFEREDACH (MURAN, MURAMES) — SEVENTH CENTURY

St. Mura McFeredach was the first Abbot and patron saint of Fahan, on the Inishowen Peninsula, in Co. Donegal. His staff and bell were held to have miraculous powers, and were greatly venerated. The year of his death in the seventh century A.D. is unknown.

13ᵀᴴ MARCH

GERALD — EIGHTH CENTURY

St. Gerald founded the monastery, and Diocese of Mayo in western Ireland. He was one of the English monks who accompanied St. Colman (18ᵗʰ February) when he retired to Ireland, following the Synod of Whitby*. St. Colman made him abbot of the English monastery he founded at Mayo, which he ruled with great success, reposing at a very advanced age A.D. 732.

KEVOCA (KENNOTHA, QUIVOCA) — SEVENTH CENTURY

An Irish or Scottish saint of whom nothing is now known with any certitude. Some claim that he is the same saint as St. Mochoemoc (*vide infra*), founder and first Abbot of Liath-Mochoemoc in Tipperary. However, in ancient Scottish Calendars St. Kevoca is listed as a female saint.

MOCHOEMOC (MOCHAEMHOG, PULCHERIUS, VULCANIUS) — SEVENTH CENTURY

The nephew of St. Ita (15ᵗʰ January), he became a monk at Bangor under St. Comgall (10ᵗʰ May), and later founded Liath-Mochoemoc. St. Mochoemoc reposed circa A.D. 655.

14TH MARCH

BONIFACE CURITAN — SEVENTH CENTURY

A Bishop of Ross in Scotland, who was very likely the leader of a group of missionaries sent from Rome to evangelise the Picts and Scots. St. Boniface Curitan is said to have founded one hundred and fifty churches. He reposed circa A.D. 650.

TALMACH — SEVENTH CENTURY

Little is known of this saint aside from a few references to him by the Bollandists*, Colgan*, and an old Life of St. Finnbarr of Cork (25th September). He seems to have been a disciple of St. Barr (25th September) at Lough Erc (present–day Guagán Barra, Co. Cork), and later founder of a monastery.

15TH March

There are no Saints of the British Isles listed on the Calendar for this date.

16TH MARCH

ABBAN — FIFTH CENTURY

A nephew of St. Ibar (23rd April), and contemporary of St. Patrick (17th March), St. Abban founded Kill-Abban Abbey in Leinster. No further information on this saint is extant.

FINIAN — SEVENTH CENTURY

A disciple of St. Columba of Iona (9th June), he is said to have been Abbot of Swords just north of Dublin. However, as is the case with many of his contemporaries, ascertaining the truth within the various and tangled traditions of his Life is impossible.

17TH MARCH

PATRICK — FIFTH CENTURY

Our father among the Saints Patrick of Ireland, Bishop of Armagh and Enlightener of Ireland, was born a Briton. Captured and brought to Ireland as a slave, he escaped and returned home. Later he returned to Ireland, bringing Christianity to its people. Although St. Patrick achieved remarkable results in spreading the Gospel, he was not the first or only missionary in Ireland, but it was St. Patrick who had the greatest influence and success in preaching the Gospel of Christ. Therefore, he is known as "The Enlightener of Ireland".

TROPARION - TONE 3

Holy Bishop Patrick,
Faithful shepherd of Christ's royal flock,
You filled Ireland with the radiance of the Gospel:

The mighty strength of the Trinity!
Now that you stand before the Saviour,
Pray that He may preserve us in faith and love!

KONTAKION - TONE 4

From slavery, you escaped to freedom in Christ's service:
He sent you to deliver Ireland from the devil's bondage.
You planted the Word of the Gospel in pagan hearts.
In your journeys and hardships, you rivalled the Apostle Paul!
Having received the reward for your labours in heaven,
Never cease to pray for the flock you have gathered on earth,
Holy Bishop Patrick!

Undoubtedly one of the best known of the Saints, his Lives and writings have been widely published in numerous languages and lands. St. Patrick was born in Britain, the son of a local *decurio* (member of a town council) called Calpornius who was also a deacon of the church, and who had a property near the village *(vicu)* of Bannavem Taburniae, the location of which is unknown. Patrick was brought up as a Christian, though in no tradition of strong piety. At the age of sixteen, he was captured by Irish pirates who took him back to Ireland where he spent six years as a herdsman. Whilst in captivity he experienced a religious conversion, and eventually received a Divine message that he was to escape. He then made his way to a port some 320 kilometres away where he found a ship whose crew he was able to convince to take him to Britain. At some point he later he went to Gaul and studied for the priesthood at Auxerre under St. Germanus (31st July). Eventually St. Patrick was consecrated bishop, and was entrusted with the mission to Ireland, succeeding St. Palladius (7th July), who had not had much success there. Though the conversion of the pagan Irish people was far from an easy task, St. Patrick persevered despite hostility, violence, and threats of death. However, in the end he baptised thousands people into Christ, founded many churches and encouraged the growth of monasticism throughout the land. By the time he established Armagh as his See, St. Patrick not only had many native priests and deacons to assist him, but other bishops as well.

St. Patrick is often depicted holding a shamrock, or with snakes fleeing from him. He used the shamrock to illustrate the doctrine of the Holy Trinity; its three leaves growing out of a single stem helped him to explain the concept of one God in three Persons. It is commonly accepted that the story of St. Patrick driving all the snakes out of Ireland has no basis in fact.

St. Patrick reposed on 17th March, though the exact year is a matter of some speculation, with dates ranging from A.D. 461 to A.D. 493. The various accounts of his last days are most likely legend, and it had been said that the place of his burial was unknown, though St. Columba of Iona (9th June) says the Holy Spirit revealed to him that St. Patrick was buried at the site of his first church in Saul, Co. Down, and a granite marker was placed at his traditional grave site in Downpatrick A.D. 1899.

18ᵀᴴ March

Edward the Martyr — Tenth Century

The holy and right-believing King Edward the Martyr succeeded his father, St. Edgar the Peaceful (8th July), as King of England, but was murdered after a reign of only a few years. As the murder was attributed to "irreligious" opponents, and Edward himself was considered a good Christian, he was glorified as St. Edward the Martyr by an English Church Council (A.D. 1001), an act which has been confirmed by the Council of Bishops of the Russian Orthodox Church Outside of Russia (Decree Nº 255, dated 6/19 September, 1979). He may also be considered a passion-bearer.

TROPARION OF ST. EDWARD THE MARTYR
TONE 4

Celebrating the newly manifest commemoration of the holy King Edward,
who shone forth of old in the virtues and suffered undeservedly we all
bow down before the Icon of his honoured countenance and in gladness cry out:
Truly Thou art wonderful in Thy Saints, O God.

St. Edward ascended to the throne at the age of thirteen. Though the eldest son of King St. Edgar the Peaceful, Edward's accession to the throne was contested by a group headed by his stepmother, Queen Elfrida, who wished her son, Ethelred the Unready, to become king instead. However, Edward's claim had more support—including that of St. Dunstan (19th May) — and was confirmed by the Witan.

Described by Theodoric Paulus as "a young man of great devotion and excellent conduct; he was wholly Catholic, good and of holy life; moreover, above all things he loved God and the Church; he was generous to the poor, a haven to the good, a champion of the Faith of Christ, a vessel full of every virtuous grace". St. Edward continued his father's policies and support for St. Dunstan's reforms. This displeased those nobles who had designs on monastic lands, and they joined with Queen Elfrida in a conspiracy to do away with the young king. On 18th March A.D. 978 the king was murdered whilst sitting on his horse outside the home of his younger brother.

Almost immediately following his martyrdom, miracles began. Following the murder, the body of the king slipped from the saddle of his horse and was dragged with one foot in the stirrup until the body fell into a stream (which was subsequently found to have healing properties — particularly for the blind) at the base of the hill upon which Corfe Castle stands. Queen Elfrida then ordered the body be hidden in a nearby hut. This hut was occupied by a woman who had been blind from birth, receiving the tenancy from the Queen as an act of charity. During the night the entire hut was filled with a most wondrous light, and, struck with awe, the woman cried out "Lord, have mercy!" and her sight was restored. The church of St. Edward at Corfe Castle, Dorset today marks the location where the hut is believed to have stood. When the Queen learned of this miracle, she ordered that the body be buried in a marsh near Wareham. However, a year later a pillar of fire was seen over the spot where the body was hidden. The locals raised the body, and, accompanied by a large group of mourners, translated the relics to a church in Wareham where they buried them in the east end of the church. The relics, which when exhumed were found to be still whole and incorrupt, were next translated to Shaftesbury Abbey where they were received by the nuns and buried with full royal honours on the north side of the altar.

During the Dissolution of the Monasteries under Henry VIII, St. Edward's relics were hidden so as to avoid desecration. In A.D. 1931, the relics were recovered by Mr. J.E. Wilson-Claridge during an archaeological excavation; their identity was confirmed by Dr. T.E.A. Stowell, an osteologist. These findings were confirmed by the Council of Bishops of the Russian Orthodox Church Outside of Russia (Decree № 255, dated 6/19 September, A.D. 1979). Mr. Wilson-Claridge donated the relics to the Russian Orthodox Church Outside Russia, which placed them in the care of the monastery of the St. Edward Brotherhood at Brookwood Cemetery, in Woking, Surrey.

EGBERT – EIGHTH CENTURY

A monk at Ripon, St. Egbert reposed circa A.D. 720. No further information on this saint is extant.

19ᵀᴴ MARCH

ALCMUND — NINTH CENTURY

He was the son of Eldred, and brother of Osred, Northumbrian kings. After years of exile amongst the Picts in Scotland St. Alcmund was martyred in Shropshire circa A.D. 800. His body was first interred at Lilleshult, in Shropshire, but was later translated to Derby, where he was patron of the town.

AUXILIUS — FIFTH CENTURY

A member of St. Patrick's mission to Ireland, St. Auxilius served as Bishop of Killossey. The year of his repose is believed to have been circa A.D. 460. There is no other reliable information extant.

LACTAN — SEVENTH CENTURY

Born near Cork in Ireland, according to tradition a miraculous spring provided the water for his Baptism. At the age of fifteen his Guardian Angel took him to St. Comgall (10ᵗʰ May) Abbot of Bangor. It is known with certainty that he did enter Bangor, and whilst there he studied under St. Lua (4ᵗʰ August). St. Lactan was then was appointed by St. Comgall to found several monasteries, presiding as founding Abbot of Achadh-Ur (present-day Freshford, Co. Kilkenny), until his repose A.D. 672.

20ᵀᴴ March

Cuthbert — Seventh Century

Our father among the saints Cuthbert of Lindisfarne, Wonder-worker of Britain, was a monastic missionary and bishop during the seventh century A.D. in Scotland and the north of England, where he is still widely venerated.

TROPARION — TONE 3

While still in your youth, you laid aside all worldly cares,
and took up the sweet yoke of Christ,
and you were shown forth in truth to be nobly radiant
in the grace of the Holy Spirit.

Therefore, God established you as a rule of faith and shepherd of His radiant flock,
Godly-minded Cuthbert, converser with angels and intercessor for men.

KONTAKION – TONE 1

Having surpassed your brethren in prayers, fasting and vigils,
you were found worthy to entertain an angel in the form of a pilgrim;
and having shown forth with humility as a bright lamp set on high,
you received the gift of working wonders.
And now as you dwell in the Heavenly Kingdom, our righteous Father Cuthbert,
intercede with Christ our God that our souls may be saved.

There are several conflicting legends regarding St. Cuthbert's early life. The general consensus is that he was a shepherd who had a vision at the moment of the death of St. Aidan (31st August), seeing that saint rising in glory to Heaven, which led him to embrace the monastic life. He was tonsured at Melrose under St. Eata (26th October), and was taught by St. Boswell (23rd February). After several years there, where he was held in awe by his fellow monks for his fasting and vigils, St. Eata selected several monks to join him and St. Cuthbert, on a journey to a new monastery at Ripon. However, due to the disagreement over the Celtic versus Roman practices of calculating the date of Pascha, they returned to Melrose. Following the Synod of Whitby*, St. Cuthbert seems to have accepted the Roman liturgical practices, and after St. Columba (9th June) and his monks left Lindisfarne, SS. Cuthbert and Eata went to Lindisfarne, where St. Cuthbert eventually became abbot. During his first years at Lindisfarne, St. Cuthbert actively continued his missionary work, travelling southward to Northumberland and Durham, though he sincerely desired the life of an anchorite. In A.D. 676 he retired to a cave, and then into a cell he built on the isolated island of Inner Farne, south of Lindisfarne. Alas, his solitude was not to last, as the king implored him to accept episcopal consecration, and St. Cuthbert was made Bishop of Lindisfarne in A.D. 684. Whilst maintaining an ascetic life, St. Cuthbert led his diocese, caring for the sick, distributing alms, and working the many miracles that earned him the title of Wonder-worker of Britain. Then in late A.D. 686, in declining health, he resigned his office and retired to his cell on Inner Farne Island where he reposed, 20th March A.D. 687. He was buried at Lindisfarne, though in the ninth century A.D. the Viking threat prompted the Lindisfarne community to move his body, which was found to be still incorrupt, to a safer site, first to Chester-le-Street, and finally to Durham. Important sanctuary rights developed early around St. Cuthbert's body, and his cult, surviving both the Scandinavian and Norman conquests, emerged as one of the most important in medieval England. His pectoral cross, portable altar, coffin-reliquary and other objects survived the destruction of his shrine in A.D. 1539-40, and were recovered when his tomb in Durham Cathedral was opened in A.D. 1827.

HERBERT — SEVENTH CENTURY

According to St. Bede the Venerable (25th May), he was a disciple of St. Cuthbert (*vide supra*), who lived as an anchorite on what is now called St. Herbert's Island in Lake Derwenwater, in the Lake District of England. He reposed on the same day as his holy master, 20th March, A.D. 687.

21ST MARCH

ENDA (ENDEUS, ENNA) — SIXTH CENTURY

The brother of St. Fanchea (1st January), St. Enda founded many of the earliest monasteries in Ireland. His principal monastery was at Killeany in the Arran Islands. SS. Kyran of Clonmacnoise (9th September) and Brendan (16th May) were amongst his disciples. St. Enda reposed circa A.D. 530.

22ND MARCH

DARERCA — FIFTH CENTURY

St. Darerca was St. Patrick's sister. Her name derived from the Irish *Diarsheare*, signifying constant or firm love, and denotes her characteristic in God's service. She is reputed to have had fifteen sons, ten of whom became bishops. The exact year of her repose is unknown to us.

FAILBHE — SEVENTH CENTURY

The brother of St. Finan of Rath (7th April), St. Failbhe was the immediate predecessor of St. Adamnán (23rd September) as Abbot of Iona. Nothing further is known of this saint.

TRIEN (TRIENAN) — FIFTH CENTURY

A disciple of St. Patrick (17th March) he served as Abbot of Killega, and was a close friend of St. Mochta (19th August). There is no further information on this saint extant.

23ʳᵈ MARCH

ETHILWALD — SEVENTH CENTURY

A monk at Ripon, St. Ethilwald lived as an anchorite on the Island of Farne for the last twelve years of his life, reposing A.D. 699.

MAIDOC (MO-MHAEDOG) — FIFTH CENTURY

An Abbot of Fiddown in southern Co. Kilkenny in Ireland, nothing further is known about him.

24ᵀᴴ MARCH

CAIMIN (CAMMIN) OF INNISKELTRA — SEVENTH CENTURY

St. Caimin lived as a hermit on an island in Lough Derg in Ireland. Many disciples were drawn to him, leading him to found a monastery and church on the island of the Seven Churches. He is said to have worked with St. Senan (8th March). A fragment of the *Psalter of St. Caimin*, copied in his own hand, is still extant.

CAIRLON (CAORLAN) — SIXTH CENTURY

An Irish abbot he later served as Archbishop of Cashel. There is a legend that he died and was restored to life by St. Daig Maccairill (18th August). When St. Cairlon had been made Archbishop of Cashel, St. Daig Maccairill placed himself and his monks under his rule.

DOMANGARD (DONARD) — FIFTH CENTURY

The patron saint of Maghera, Co. Down, St. Domangard lived as an anchorite on the mountain now called Slieve-Donard, and reposed towards the end of the fifth century A.D.

MACARTAN (MACARTIN, MACCARTHEN) – SIXTH CENTURY

St. Macartan was an early disciple and faithful companion of St. Patrick (17th March), who consecrated him first Bishop of Clogher. According to legend St. Patrick gave him his own pastoral staff upon his consecration. There is no further information on this saint extant.

25TH MARCH

ALFWOLD (ÆLFWOLD) – ELEVENTH CENTURY

A monk at Winchester, St. Alfwold was known for his great devotion to SS. Swithun (2nd July) and Cuthbert (20th March). He was consecrated Bishop of Sherborne in A.D. 1045, governing that See with great zeal and prudence until his repose A.D. 1058.

KENNOCHA (KYLE, ENOCH) – ELEVENTH CENTURY

She was a nun of noble Scottish birth at a monastery in Fife. She was held in great veneration in Scotland, especially in Strathclyde. She reposed A.D. 1007. No further information on this saint is extant.

26TH MARCH

GARBHAN — SEVENTH CENTURY

Nothing certain is known about this Irish saint, though he seems to have left his name to the town of Dungarvan (*Dún Garbháin*) in Co. Waterford, Ireland.

MOCHELLOC (CELLOG, MOTTELOG, MOTALOGUS) — SEVENTH CENTURY

The patron saint of Kilmallock (*Cill Mocheallóg*) in Co. Limerick, there are no reliable details of his life extant.

SINCHEALL — FIFTH CENTURY

A disciple of St. Patrick (17th March), he founded the monastery of Killeigh in Co. Offaly Ireland. At its peak, there were one hundred and fifty monks at the monastery. There is no further information on this saint extant.

27TH MARCH

ALKELD (ATHILDA) — TENTH CENTURY

There are two churches in Yorkshire dedicated to this saint about whom nothing is known save for an ancient painting showing her being strangled by Danish pirates. This event may safely be dated to the tenth century A.D.

SUAIRLECH — EIGHTH CENTURY

An Abbot of Fore in Westmeath known for his zeal, he was later consecrated first Bishop of that See. St. Suairlech reposed circa A.D. 750.

28TH MARCH

There are no Saints of the British Isles listed on the Calendar for this date.

29TH MARCH

GLADYS — FIFTH CENTURY

This Welsh saint was a daughter of the famous St. Brychan of Brycheiniog (6th June), the wife of St. Gwynllyw (*vide infra*), and mother of St. Cadoc (24th January). There are no further reliable details of her life extant.

GWYNLLYW (WOOLLOS) — FIFTH CENTURY

Gwynllyw Milwr or Gwynllyw Farfog, known in English as Woolos the Warrior or Woolos the Bearded (Latin: Gundleus, Gundleius or Gwenleue), was the King of Gwynllwg in South Wales and the legendary founder and patron saint of the City of Newport. According to Lives written some six hundred years after his repose, St. Gwynllyw Milwr was a feared warlord, raider and associate of King Arthur. He later found religion, quite possibly under the influence of his son, St. Cadoc (24th January) and wife St. Gladys (*vide supra*), and became a hermit, at the location where St. Woollos Cathedral in Newport was later built. St. Gwynllyw reposed circa A.D. 500.

LASAR (LASSAR, LASSERA) — SIXTH CENTURY

An Irish monastic St. Lasar was a niece of St. Fortchern (17th February). Limited details of her life, of uncertain reliability, are provided by the Bollandists*, as well as Colgan*. From these it is known that she spent her early years in the care of SS. Finnian (7th April) and Kieran (9th September) at Clonard, before entering an unknown monastery.

30TH MARCH

FERGUS — SIXTH CENTURY

He was a Bishop of Downpatrick in Co. Down in Ireland. Though he has always been held in great veneration, the details of his life are uncertain, and it is even possible that he was the same man as St. Fergus of Scotland (27th November), who flourished in the eighth century A.D.

OSBURGH (OSBURGA) — ELEVENTH CENTURY

An Abbess, and according to some sources the first of the convent founded at Coventry by King Canute. There are no particulars about her extant.

TOLA — EIGHTH CENTURY

Little is known about this saint, other than that he was originally a hermit at Tola, Co. Meath. He built a monastery for his many disciples, and eventually was consecrated Bishop of Clonard. He is believed to have reposed circa A.D. 733.

31ˢᵀ MARCH

There are no Saints of the British Isles listed on the Calendar for this date.

APPENDIX – I

ABERDEEN BREVIARY

Edited by William Elphinstone, the *Aberdeen Breviary* is a 16th century Scottish Catholic service book, which has been described as the "Sarum Office in Scottish form". For our purposes, it is notable for its accounts of a variety of Scottish saints.

BARING-GOULD

The Revd. Sabine Baring Baring-Gould, MA († A.D. 1924) was a Church of England priest, novelist, antiquarian, hagiographer, and eclectic scholar. He is also remembered as a writer of hymns, including "Onward Christian Soldiers". An exceedingly prolific writer, his bibliography currently stands at over 1,240 publications, and his sixteen-volume *The Lives of the Saints* is a treasure of hagiographic information.

BUTLER

The Revd. Fr. Alban Butler († A.D. 1773) was an English Roman Catholic priest. After extensive studies and travel throughout the Continent, in 1756-9 he published *The Lives of the Fathers, Martyrs and other principal Saints, compiled from original Monuments and other authentic records, illustrated with the remarks of judicious modern critics and historians.* In this work, the Lives of over 1,600 saints are arranged according to the Church calendar, and although though their chief purpose was edification, and history and legend are not differentiated, they remain a monumental work. To this day *Butler's Lives of the Saints* remains a foundational work for hagiographic research, reference, and education.

COLGAN

John Colgan, OFM (†c. A.D. 1657) was an Irish Franciscan and noted hagiographer and historian. Following studies at the Irish Franciscan College of St. Anthony of Padua in Louvain, where he served briefly as a Professor of Theology, but soon turned to Irish studies and wrote his six volume Irish ecclesiastical history. The last four volumes (*Acta Sanctorum Hiberniae*) cover the lives of Irish Saints. The second volume of the series entitled *Acta Triadis Thaumaturgae* (The Acts of a Wonder-Working Triad) cover the lives of SS. Patrick, Brigid of Kildare, and Columba. For a long time the *Triadis Thaumaturgae* was nearly the only source of information on St. Patrick.

DE EXCIDIO ET CONQUESTU BRITANNIÆ

De Excidio et Conquestu Britanniæ (On the Ruin and Conquest of Britain) is a work by the sixth-century A.D. British cleric St. Gildas the Wise. A sermon in three parts, it condemns the acts of St. Gildas' contemporaries, both secular and religious, whom he blames for the dire state of affairs in sub-Roman Britain. *De Excidio* is one of the most important sources for the history of fifth and sixth century A.D. Britain, as it is the only significant source for the period written by a near contemporary of the people and events described.

HISTORIA ECCLESIASTICA GENTIS ANGLORUM – VEN. BEDE

Believed to have been completed in A.D. 731, this work is considered to be one of the most important original references on Anglo-Saxon history. St. Bede the Venerable's (25th May) *Historia ecclesiastica gentis Anglorum (Ecclesiastical History of the English People)* is a history of England and of the Christian Churches in England, and has played a key role in the development of an English national identity.

Divided into five books (approximately 400 pages total), the *Historia* covers the history of England, both ecclesiastical and political, from the time of Julius Caesar to the date of the *Historia's* completion (A.D. 731). The first twenty-one chapters, covering the period before the mission of Augustine, are compiled from the works of earlier writers including Orosius, Gildas, Prosper of Aquitaine, the letters of Pope St. Gregory the Dialogist and others, with the insertion of legends and traditions. After AD 596, documentary sources that St. Bede the Venerable (25th May) took pains to obtain throughout England and from Rome are used, as well as oral testimony, which he referred to along with critical consideration of its authenticity.

IONA

In A.D. 563 St. Columba of Iona (9th June), exiled from his native Ireland, founded a monastery on this small island of the Inner Hebrides. Called in Gaelic *Í Chaluim Cille*, *Í* of St. Columba variously spelt Hi, Hy or I. The modern form of the name derives from an error in copying St. Adamnán of Iona's (23rd September) adjectival form 'Ioua Insula' in his Life of St. Columba. From Iona Orthodox Christianity spread to the rest of Scotland. Numerous martyrs and other saints were produced from Iona, including not only St. Columba, but also St. Aidan of Lindisfarne (31st August) and several others. Many believe that the *Book of Kells* was produced on Iona at this time. The monastery survived until the Protestant Reformation.

LINDISFARNE

Beginning with St. Aidan's (31ˢᵗ August) arrival from Iona in A.D. 635, Lindisfarne quickly became a missionary centre and episcopal see, and a large number of churches were founded by its monks from Edinburgh to the Humber and beyond. Among those educated in the monastery were SS. Chad (2ⁿᵈ March), Cedd (26ᵗʰ October), Egbert (24ᵗʰ April), and Wilfrid (12ᵗʰ October). Following the Synod of Whitby* (A.D. 664) the Scoto-Irish monks, along with some of their English brethren, withdrew to Iona, as they disagreed with the Roman liturgical practices adopted at the Synod, and from that time the monastery looked towards Rome. St. Cuthbert's (20ᵗʰ March) association with it added to its celebrity. In A.D. 793 and again in A.D. 875 the monastery, and church were pillaged by the Danes, and the monks fled. Eardulf († A.D. 900), the last of the 16 bishops, fixed his see in A.D. 875 at Chester-le-Street, but it was transferred to Durham in A.D. 995. From A.D. 1082 until the Dissolution there was continuous monastic life on the island.

MARTYROLOGIUM HIERONYMIANUM

The *Martyrology Hieronymianum* (Martyrology of St. Jerome) is the oldest surviving comprehensive martyrology, and the ultimate source of all later Western martyrologies. Whilst the title attributes authorship to St. Jerome, the *Martyrologium Hieronymianum* contains a reference to him derived from the opening chapter of his *Vita Malchi* (A.D. 392) in which St. Jerome states his intention to write a history of the saints and martyrs from the apostolic times. The *Martyrology*

Hieronymianum is believed to have been compiled in the late sixth century A.D. by monks in Gaul from calendars or martyrologies originating in Rome, Africa, the Christian east, and local sources.

PASCHAL CONTROVERSY

Among the many controversies in the early Church over the complex question as to how to calculate the date of Pascha, was the use by the Celtic Churches of their own method of computation, which led to a long quarrel in the British Isles after the arrival of the Roman missionaries. Even a cursory overview of this question is beyond the scope of this book; in fact, the subject deserves a book, or books, of its own. However, in summary, the question facing Church in the British Isles — Celtic v. Roman practice for the calculation of Pascha — was that the Celtic Church had its own methods of calculating the date which differed from them Roman method of calculation. This resulted, in A.D. 651, in Queen Eanfleda, who followed the Roman rule, keeping Palm Sunday, and fasting on the same day that her husband, Oswiu, King of Northumbria, was celebrating Pascha. The issue was settled at the Synod of Whitby* *(vide infra)* A.D. 664 in favour of the Roman practice, though Celtic parts of the British Isles, especially Scotland, Wales, and Cornwall held out for another fifty to one hundred years.

PELAGIANISM

Pelagius, a British biblical scholar and theologian lived in Rome in the late fourth and early fifth centuries. In his writings, Pelagius took the position that man can take the initial and fundamental steps towards salvation solely through his own efforts. In Pelagius' view, the role of Jesus is merely that of "setting a good example" and divine grace has no role in man's salvation. Initially his writings were condemned by St. Augustine of Hippo; then Pelagius was excommunicated in A.D. 417 by Pope Innocent I, and his views were subsequently condemned by a series of Church councils. However, the issues of human freedom and divine grace have remained central topics of debate throughout the history of Christian theology.

SOCIÉTÉ DES BOLLANDISTES (THE BOLLANDISTS)

The Bollandists are an association of scholars, philologists, and historians (originally all Jesuits) who, since the early seventeenth century, have studied hagiography and the cult of the saints in Christianity. Their most important publication has been the *Acta Sanctorum*. They are named after Father Jean van Bolland (or Bollandus † A.D. 1665) who was prefect of studies at the Jesuit college of Mechelen and founded the group.

SYNOD OF WHITBY

A significant local council, the Synod of Whitby led to the liturgical and administrative unification of the Church in England. Called by King Oswiu of Northumbria, the synod was held in A.D. 664 at Whitby Abbey. Initially the matters in dispute were fairly minor, the main controversies being what style of tonsure clerics should wear — the Roman coronal tonsure, or the Celtic style of shaving the whole head in front of a line drawn from ear to ear, as well as how to calculate the date of Pascha (*vide Paschal Controversy supra*). However, the final outcome of the synod was that Roman, rather than Celtic, practices would have ascendency over the entire north of England. The matter came to a head one spring when the king, who followed the Celtic practice, was feasting at Pascha, while the queen, who followed Roman practice, was still fasting for Lent. The advocate for Celtic practices was St. Coleman of Iona (18th February), whilst St. Wilfrid (12th October) advocated for the Roman practices. In the end, the Roman practices were adopted, and those clerics and monastics who would not change withdrew to Iona and later to Ireland. Though St. Bede the Venerable (25th May) describes the proceedings in great detail, and made the Synod of Whitby the turning-point of his history: until A.D. 664 Christianity came to the English through different traditions; from A.D. 664 the trend is towards unity and orthodoxy. However, the *Anglo-Saxon Chronicle*, makes no mention of the synod.

APPENDIX - II — DECREE ON THE VENERATION OF ANCIENT SAINTS OF THE WEST

Decree No. 223, 23rd April, A.D. 1953.

Archbishop St. John of Shanghai and San Francisco

SOJOURNING in the diaspora in countries where, in olden times, holy God-pleasers laboured and were celebrated for their suffering or other ascetic struggles and have been revered by the Orthodox Christian Church from ancient times, it is fitting for us to honour and turn to them, without at the same time growing cold towards those holy God-pleasers to whom we have previously turned in prayer. In various places of ancient Gaul (today's France) and other countries of Western Europe, the sacred remains of martyrs from the first centuries and following who were confessors of the Orthodox faith have been preserved to the present. We call on clergy to commemorate at divine services – at the litiya and in other prayers – those God-pleasers who are the patrons of the place or country where the service is taking place and are especially revered, as well as at the dismissal. In particular, in Paris Hieromartyr Dionysius, Venerable Genevieve, and Venerable Clodoald should be commemorated; in Lyons, Hieromartyr Irenaeus; in Marseille, Martyr Victor and Venerable [John] Cassian; in Toulouse, Hieromartyr Saturninus, Bishop of Toulouse; in Tours, Holy Hierarch Martin. In cases of uncertainty or confusion, we advise you turn to us for clarification and guidance. The flock is likewise called upon to honour these God-pleasers.

BIBLIOGRAPHY/REFERENCES

"Saints of the British Isles." Archdiocese of Thyateira and Great Britain, 2005. Web.

Baring-Gould, S. *The Lives of the Saints.* London: Hodges, 1875. Print.

Bede, and A. M. Sellar. *Bede's Ecclesiastical History of the English People;.* London: G. Bell and Sons, 1917. Print.

Blew, William. *Breviarium Aberdonense.* London: Toovey, 1854. Print.

Bolland, Johannes, Jean Baptiste Carnandet, and Godefridus Henschenius. *Acta Sanctorum Quotquot Toto Orbe Coluntur, Vel a Catholicis Scriptoribus Celebrantur Quae Ex Latinis Et Graecis, Aliarumque Gentium Antiquis Monumentis.* Bruxelles: Culture Et Civilisation, 1965. Print.

The Book of Saints: A Dictionary of Servants of God Canonised by the Catholic Church : Extracted from the Roman & Other Martyrologies. [Whitefish, MT]: Kessinger, 2001. Print.

Butler, Alban. *The Lives of the Fathers, Martyrs, and Other Principal Saints Compiled from Original Monuments, and Other Authentic Records: Illustrated with the Remarks of Judicious Modern Critics and Historians. By the Rev. Alban Butler. The Second Edition, Corrected and Enlarged from the Author's Own Manuscript. In Twelve Volumes. ...* Dublin: Printed by J. Chambers, for John Morris, 1779. Print.

Colgan, John. *Acta Sanctorum Veteris Et Maioris Scotiae.* Louvain: Apud Everardum De Witte, 1645. Print.

Colgan, John. *Triadis Thaumaturgae Seu Divorum Patricii, Columbae Et Brigidae ... Acta ... Collecta, Scholiis & Commentariis Illustrata, & Pluribus Appendicibus Aucta; Complectitur Tomus Secundus Sacrarum Ejusdem Insulae Antiquitatum, Nunc Primum in Lucem Prodiens.* Louvain: Coenestenius, 1647. Print.

Cross, F. L., and Elizabeth A. Livingstone. *The Oxford Dictionary of the Christian Church.* London: Oxford UP, 1974. Print.

Dunbar, Agnes Baillie Cunninghame. *A Dictionary of Saintly Women.* London: Bell, 1904. Print.

Forbes, A. P. *Kalendars of Scottish Saints: With Personal Notices of Those of Alba, Laudonia, & Strathclyde : An Attempt to Fix the Districts of Their Several Missions and the Churches Where They Were Chiefly Had in Remembrance.* Edinburgh: Edmonston and Douglas, 1872. Print.

Gildas, and J. A. Giles. *On the Ruin of Britain = (De Excidio Britanniae).* [United States]: Dodo, 2012. Print.

Herbermann, Charles. *The Catholic Encyclopedia.* New York: Appleton, 1907. Print.

Jérôme, Rossi Giovanni Battista De, and Louis Duchesne. *Martyrologium Hieronymianum...*Bruxellis: n.p., 1894. Print.

Lanigan, John. *An Ecclesiastical History of Ireland: From the First Introduction of Christianity among the Irish, to the Beginning of the Thirteenth Century : Compiled from the Works of the Most Esteemed Authors ... Who Have Written and Published on Matters Connected with the Irish Church; and from Irish Annals and Other Authentic Documents Still Existing in Manuscript.* Dublin: Printed by D. Graisberry, 1822. Print.

"Latin Saints of the Orthodox Patriarchate of Rome." *Latin Saints of the Orthodox Patriarchate of Rome.* Fr Andrew Phillips, 2 Oct. 2003. Web.

"Lives of the Saints." *Orthodox Church in America.* Orthodox Church in America, 1996. Web.

Maguire, Cathal MacMaghnusa, Rory O'Cassidy, W. M. Hennessy, and Batholomew MacCarthy. *Annala Uladh = Annals of Ulster : Otherwise, Annala Senait, Annals of Senat : A Chronicle of Irish Affairs.* Dublin: Printed for H.M. Stationery Off., by A. Thom, 1887. Print.

O'Hanlon, John. *Lives of the Irish Saints: With Special Festivals, and the Commemorations of Holy Persons, Compiled from Calenders, Martyrologies, and Various Sources, Relating to the Ancient Church History of Ireland.* Dublin: James Duffy and Sons, 1873. Print.

Plummer, Charles. *Miscellanea Hagiographica Hibernica; Vitae Adhuc Ineditae Sanctorum MacCreiche, Naile, Cranat,.* Bruxelles: Société Des Bollandistes, 1925. Print.

ÓRiain, Pádraig. *Corpus Genealogiarum Sanctorum Hiberniae.* Dublin: Dublin Inst. for Advanced Studies, 1985. Print.

Smith, William, and Henry Wace. *A Dictionary of Christian Biography, Literature, Sects and Doctrines: Being a Continuation of "The Dictionary of the Bible"* [Whitefish, MT]: Kessinger Pub., 2005. Print.

Stanton, Richard. *A Menology of England and Wales; Or, Brief Memorials of the Ancient British and English Saints Arranged According to the Calendar, Together with the Martyrs of the 16th and 17th Centuries;.* London: Burns & Oates, 1887. Print.

INDEX

Abban of Kill-Abban, St..... 115, 185
Aberdaron.................................... 33
Aberdeen Breviary 69, 223
Aberdeen, Bishop of................... 38
Achadh-Ur, Abbot of................ 195
Acta Sanctorum Hiberniae ....
.... *See* Colgan, John
Acta Triadis Thaumaturgae ....
.... *See* Colgan, John
Adamnán of Iona, St. ....
.... 89, 203, 225
Adamnan, St. 89
Adrian and Companions, St...... 159
Adrian, St................................. 152
Áedan of Ferns, St. 85, 89, 90
Ælflæd, St. .... *See* Elfleda, St.
Ælfwold, St. ....*See* Alfwold, St.
Ængus, King.............................. 161
Ængus, St.................................. 175
Æthelberht of Kent, King 95
Aidan of Lindisfarne, St. ....
......127, 129, 153, 198, 225, 226
Aidan, St. ...... *See* Áedan of Ferns, St.
Alban, St. 105
Albert of Cashel, St...................... 37
Albert, St.....................................
.... *See* Ethelbert of Kent, St.
Alchfrid of Northumberland 163
Alcmund, St. 195
Alcuin 133
Aldate, St. 99
Alfred, King 137
Alfric, St..................................... 71
Alfwold, St. 209
Alkeld, St. 213
Allan, St. ....*See* Elian, St.
All-Faranna ....*See* Alterna

Alnoth, St. 147
Alphege the Elder, St................. 177
Altarnun 158
Alterna...................................... 123
Ambleteuse 34
Ambra Choluim Kille................. 85
Andrew, St. 70
Anglesey.................... 33, 49, 77, 94
Anglo-Saxons 95
Angus, St....................*See* Ængus, St.
Anianus, St. .... *See* Eingan, St.
Annals of Ulster 123, 157
Annandale 152
Antrim 37
Apostle of East Anglia 167
Arbroath 67
Ardagh and Clonmacnois, Diocese
of.. 103
Ardagh, Bishop of..................... 103
Ardcarne, Bishop of.................. 167
Armagh 161, 189
Armagh, Archbishop of.............. 43
Armagh, Bishop of..................... 187
Armagh, Diocese of 94
Armoy....................................... 133
Arran Islands 201
Arthur, King 217
Asaph of Wales, St....................... 57
Athelhelm, St.............................. 37
Athelm, St........... *See* Athelhelm, St.
Athelney, Abbot of 137
Athelstan, King..................... 37, 65
Athilda, St.................. *See* Alkeld, St.
Audrey, St. 119
Augulus, St............................... 105
Augurius, St. .... *See* Augulus, St.

Augustine of Canterbury, St............
........34, 95, 127, 141, 143, 225
Aule of Normandy, St.....................
.... *See* Ouil of Normandy, St.
Aule, St. .... *See* Augulus, St.
Auxerre 188
Auxilius, St. 195
Baldred, St. 163
Balla, Abbey............................... 23
Ballymakeera............................. 114
Ballyvourney 114
Balther, St. .... *See* Baldred, St.
Bandry 173
Bangor ....
..27, 33, 109, 128, 149, 150, 179
Bangor Abbey 23
Bangor, Abbot of 195
Bantry 83
Barachias, St. .... *See* Berach St.
Bardney...................................... 98
Bardsey, Abbot of 56
Baring-Gould 149, 223
Barking Abbey 78
Barnstaple 35
Barr, St. 181
Barrow 154
Bavaria 37
Bawnboy 89
Beatus, St. .... *See* Beoadh, St.
Bede the Venerable, St. ....
    23, 47, 55, 60, 77, 95, 111, 113,
    117, 139, 154, 171, 199, 225,
    229
Benedict Biscop, St. 47, 165
Beoadh, St. 167
Berach, St.................................... 123
Berachius, St. .... *See* Berach, St.
Berethwald, St.......*See* Brithwald, St.
Bertha (Queen).................... 99, 141
Bertha of France 143
Bilfrid, St. 163
Billfrith, St. .... *See* Bilfrid, St.
Birnstan, St. 177
Blaithmaic, St. 55

Blaithmale, St. ..... *See* Blaithmaic, St.
Blath, St. 85
Blathmac, St. .... *See* Blaithmaic, St.
Bodfari, Abbot of 165
Bodmin Moor............................ 158
Boisil, St. .... *See* Boswell, St.
Bolcan, St. 133
Bollandists ....
........*See* Société des Bollandistes
Boniface Curitan, St............ 90, 181
Boniface, St. 105
Book of Kells............................. 226
Bosa, St. 171
Boswell, St. 139, 198
Boulogne 34
Brannoc, St............................ 35, 65
Branwalader, St. ....
....................*See* Branwallader, St.
Branwalator, St. ....
....................*See* Branwallader, St.
Branwallader, St. 65
Braughton.....................................35
Breaca, St. 93, 137
Brelade, St. ......*See* Branwallader, St.
Brendan the Voyager, St..................
...........................55, 59, 65, 201
Breward, St. ......*See* Branwallader, St.
Bride, St.....*See* Brigid of Kildare, St.
Bridget, St..*See* Brigid of Kildare, St.
Briga, St. .. *See* Brigid of Kilbride, St.
Brigid of Ireland ....
.............*See* Brigid of Kildare, St.
Brigid of Kilbride, St. 69
Brigid of Kildare, St............................
....23, 55, 69, 85, 91, 92, 93, 224
Brigid of Killbrige, St........................
.... *See* Brigid of Kilbride, St.
Brihtwald, St.........*See* Brithwald, St.
Britain........... 35, 75, 188, 197, 199
Brithwald, St......................... 41, 71
Brittany.......................................
    24, 33, 35, 56, 65, 75, 95, 110,
    137, 158
Brookwood Cemetery............... 193

Brychan of Brycheiniog, King St......
............35, 75, 77, 87, 165, 217
Budoc, St.................................... 158
Burghcastle................................ 60
Burgundy 168
Butler 23, 141, 223
Cadfan, St. 33, 56, 158
Cadoc, St...................75, 123, 217
Cadvaci, St. .... See Cadoc, St.
Cadwalla, King............................ 99
Cædmon, St....................... 113, 114
Cædmon's Hymn of Creation 114
Caellainn, St. 97
Caimin of Inniskeltra, St. 207
Cainder, St............. See Cannera, St.
Cairlon, St................................. 207
Calendar of Cashel 69
Cambrai....................................... 99
Cammin, St................................
......See Caimin of Inniskeltra, St.
Cannera, St. 83
Canterbury................................
...............37, 47, 53, 71, 99, 168
Canterbury Cathedral................ 143
Canterbury, Archbishop of.............
.........................iii, iv, 37, 41, 95
Cantigernus, St. ....
...........See Kentigern Mungo, St.
Canute, King.............................. 219
Caoilfionn, St. ......See Caellainn, St.
Caorlan, St.............. See Cairlon, St.
Caradog...................................... 119
Carmarthenshire.......................... 87
Carnarvon.................................... 56
Caron, St.................................... 161
Carse of Gowrie........................... 90
Carthage the Elder, St................ 161
Carthage the Younger, St........... 161
Cashel 37, 173
Cashel, Archbishop of 207
Cassidus, Abbot.......................... 169
Castor.. 163
Cathmael, St. ....See Cadoc, St.
Cathuberis, Abbess 93

Cavan.. 89
Ceadda, St. ....See Chad, St.
Ceara, St. ....See Cera, St.
Cedd, St............. 127, 153, 154, 226
Cele-Christ, St. 157
Cellog, St. ....See Mochelloc, St.
Celtic ....
86, 127, 129, 130, 198, 227, 228
Ceolwulf, St. 55
Cera, St. 31
Chad, St............ 153, 154, 159, 226
Channel Islands........................... 65
Chatteris 119
Chester 97
Chester Cathedral 97
Chester-le-Street................. 199, 226
Chier, St. ....See Kiara, St.
Church of England.................... 223
Ciar, St..........................See Cera, St.
Ciaran, St...................See Kieran, St.
Cill Dara .... See Kildare
Cill Íde......................See Killeedy
Cill Mocheallóg ....See Kilmallock
Cill Naile 81
Cille MoGhlasaidh .....See Kinglassie
Cinna, St.................................... 93
Cinnia, St................................... 93
Cior, St. ....See Cera, St.
Ciwa, St. ....See Kigwe, St.
Ciwg, St.......................See Kigwe, St.
Clogher, Bishop of..................... 208
Clonard........................61, 89, 217
Clonard, Bishop of 219
Clondrohid............................... 114
Clonenagh 128
Clonenagh, Abbot of................. 175
Clonmacnoise............................. 59
Clonmacnoise, Abbot of 133
Clonmore 108
Clovis II 60
Clusin-Coirpte ...... See Termonbarry
Clwyd................................. 49, 119
Cnobheresburg........................... 60
Coellan, St. 36

Coldingham.................................. 89
Coleman of Iona, St. 229
Colgan, John..............................
..................69, 79, 181, 217, 224
Colgan, St. 133, 157
Colman of Armagh, St. 161
Colman of Lindisfarne, St..............
.... 129, 179
Colman of Lismore, St. 73
Columba of Iona, St. ....
27, 33, 55, 77, 81, 85, 91, 92,
109, 123, 129, 141, 152, 154,
185, 189, 198, 224, 225
Columba, St............................... 128
Comgall, St. ....
..........23, 27, 128, 150, 179, 195
Comgan, St. 36, 41, 147
Comnatan, St. .... *See* Connat, St.
Conan, St................................... 79
Conis 103
Connat, St. 23
Connaught..............................
.... 23, 59, 67, 85, 123, 129
Connor, Bishop of...................... 33
Conran, St. 121
Constantine, Prince................... 171
Constantine, St........................... 171
Corfe Castle............................... 192
Cork.............. 67, 83, 114, 169, 195
Cornwall..............................
33, 49, 65, 77, 93, 95, 97, 123,
137, 158, 162, 227
Council of Bishops of the Russian
Orthodox Church Outside of
Russia.......................... 191, 193
Coventry 219
Crewenna, St. 93
Cronan Beg, St. 36
Cronan the Wise, St. 109
Cronan, St. .... *See* Cuaran, St.
Crowan 93
Crowland 38
Cuan, St...................................... 23
Cuaran, St................................ 109

Culross.......................................51
Cumberland 109
Cumbria 50, 51
Cumine the White, St. 141
Cunedda.................................... 109
Curvinus, St..............*See* Cuaran, St.
Cuthbert of Lindisfarne, St. ....
..........................*See* Cuthbert, St.
Cuthbert, St................................
107, 111, 117, 139, 197, 198,
199, 209, 226
Cuthman, St. 107
Cwick, St. .... *See* Kigwe, St.
Cybi, St. 94, 158
Cyndeyrn, St................................
.... *See* Kentigern Mungo, St.
Cyneburgh, Cyneswith and Tibba,
SS.. 163
Cyneburgh, St............................
See Cyneburgh, Cyneswith and
Tibba, SS.
Cyneswith, St..............................
See Cyneburgh, Cyneswith and
Tibba, SS.
Cynibil, St................................ 154
Cynibild, St. ....*See* Cynibil, St.
Cyra St. ....*See* Cera St.
Daig Maccairill, St. 207
Daimhinis Island..............................
.... *See* Devenish Island
Dallán Forchella, St. ....
.................*See* Dallán Forgaill, St.
Dallán Forgaill, St.................. 85, 89
Dallán of Cluain Dalláin, St............
.................*See* Dallán Forgaill, St.
Damian.......................................53
Danish Invasions 92, 97, 137
Dardulacha, St..............................
.... *See* Darlugdach, St.
Darerca, St. 103, 203
Darlugdach, St..............................93
David of Wales, St............................
34, 67, 89, 110, 120, 151, 154,
157, 169

De Excidio et Conquestu Britanniæ 171, 224
Deifer, St. 165
Denbighshire 165
Derby 195
Derkan, Bishop 133
Derlugdach, St. ....*See* Darlugdach, St
Dermot, St. 43
Derry 27
Deusdedit, St. 53
Devenish Island 81
Devon 35
Devonshire.................................... 105
Dewi Ddyfrwr ....*See* David of Wales, St.
Dewi Sant.....*See* David of Wales, St.
Diarmaid, St............*See* Dermot, St.
Diarmis, St. ....*See* Dermot, St.
Dillo, St......................*See* Teio, St.
Dillon, St. ....*See* Teio, St.
Dima, St. ....*See* Diman, St.
Diman, St...................................... 33
Dimas, St. ....*See* Diman, St.
Diocletian 105
Disert-Nairbre 89
Dissolution of the Monasteries....... .... 193, 226
Dochau, St. ....*See* Dochow, St.
Dochow, St. 123
Dockoe, St...............*See* Dochow, St.
Docmæl, St. ....*See* Dochow, St.
Docus, St...................*See* Cadoc, St.
Dogmæl, St. ....*See* Dochow, St.
Dogwyn, St..............*See* Dochow, St.
Dol, Diocese of 65
Domangard, St............................. 207
Dominic, St......*See* Modomnock, St.
Domnoc, St......*See* Modomnock, St.
Donard, St. .... *See* Domangard, St.
Donat, St..................................... 33
Donegal............................... 81, 177
Doon.. 27
Dorset 65, 193

Downpatrick........................ 92, 189
Downpatrick, Bishop of............. 219
Drumlane...................................... 89
Dryburgh 100
Dublin 90, 92, 123, 185
Dubricius, St...................... 110, 152
Dubritius, St. 110
Dumbarton 100
Dún Garbháin ....*See* Dungarvan
Dunchaid O'Braoin, St.............. 59
Dundalk... 92
Dungarvan 211
Dunstan, St.... 37, 39, 149, 177, 192
Dunwich 168
Dunwich, Diocese of 77
Dunwyd .... *See* Donat, St.
Durham 117, 163, 198, 226
Durham Cathedral 199
Dwnawd.................................... 149
Dwynwen, St.............................. 77
Dyfed 161
Dyfnog, St. 119
Eanfleda, Queen 227
East Anglia............. 59, 60, 77, 168
Eata, St............................. 139, 198
Ebba, St....................................... 89
Ecclefechan 67
Ecclesiastical History of the English People.................................. ... *See* *Historia Ecclesiastica Gentis Anglorum*
Edfrith, St. 163
Edgar the Peaceful, King St. 191, 192
Edinburgh.................................... 226
Edward the Martyr, St. 191
Edward the Peaceful, King........ 111
Egbert, St. 139, 193, 226
Eigrad, St. 33
Eilan, St. .... *See* Elian, St.
Eingan, St. 109
Einion, St................. *See* Eingan, St.
Eldred, King............................... 195
Eleutherius, Pope St. 23

Elfleda, St. 107, 111
Elfrida, Queen 192
Elian ap Erbin, St. 49, 50
Elian, St. 49
Eloan, St. 50
Elphinstone, William 223
Elvan and Mydwyn, SS. 23
Elwin, St. 137
Ely 119
Enda, St. 24, 201
Endeus, St. .... *See* Enda, St.
Eneon, St. .... *See* Eingan, St.
England..
    33, 37, 39, 47, 50, 77, 98, 99,
    127, 137, 149, 153, 154, 163,
    168, 197, 199
English Menology.......................... 123
Enlightener of Ireland 187
Enna, St. .... *See* Enda, St.
Enoch, St. .... *See* Kennocha, St.
Enodoch, St. 165
Eochaid Forchella, ... St.
    ....*See* Dallán Forgaill, St.
Eochod, St. 77
Eosterwine, St. 165
Erard, St. 37
Erbin, St. 50
Erbyn, St. .... *See* Erbin, St.
Ercnacta, St. .... *See* Ergnad, St.
Erconbert of Kent, King 119
Ergnad, St. 37
Erme, St. .... *See* Erbin, St.
Ermenburga 61
Ermenburga, St. 139
Ermengild, St. ..... *See* Ermenhild, St.
Ermenhild, St. 97, 119
Ermenilda, St. ..... *See* Ermenhild, St.
Erth 93
Erth, St. 97
Ervan, St. .... *See* Erbin, St.
Ethelbert of Kent, King St. ....
    .... 141, 143
Ethelburga, St. 78
Etheldred, St. 119

Etheldreda of Ely, St. 78, 97, 119
Ethelina, St. 130
Ethelred the Unready 192
Ethelred, King 97
Ethelwold, St. 117, 147, 149
Ethenia and Fidelmia, SS. 45
Ethilwald, St. 205
Ethilwold, St. 117
Euchadius, St. .... *See* Eochod, St.
Eudelme, St. .... *See* Ethelina, St.
Exeter...65
Exeter Martyrology 107
Fáelchú mac Dorbbéni ..... *See* Voloc
Fahan.. 177
Failbhe the Little, St. 173
Failbhe, St.................................... 203
Faile, St. ....*See* Foila, St.
Falkirk.. 100
Fallena, St. ....*See* Foila, St.
Fanchea, St. 24, 201
Farannan, St. 123
Faughart.......................................92
Fechin, St.....................................67
Félire Óengusso ....
    .... *See* *Martyrology of Ængus*
Felix of Dunwich, St.... 77, 167, 168
Felixkirk...................................... 168
Felixstowe 168
Feock, St. 95
Fergna, St.................................... 154
Fergus of Scotland, St............... 219
Fergus, St. 219
Fermanagh............................ 24, 81
Fermoy...67
Ferns...89
Ferns, Bishop of 89
Ferns, Diocese of 89
Fiace of Leinster, St. 61
Fiddown..................................... 205
Fife.......................... 69, 83, 152, 209
Fillan, St. ....*See* Foellan, St.
Finan of Rath, St. 203
Finan, St. 127

Fingar, Phiala and Companions, SS. 97
Finian, St. 61, 89, 129, 185
Finlag, St. ....See Finlugh, St.
Finlugh, St. 27
Finnian, St. 217
Fintan Munnu, St. 31
Fintan, St. 27, 59, 128
Firth of Forth 51, 152, 159, 163
Fleury 149
Flora, St..................See Blath, St.
Fobar................... See Fore
Foellan, St. 36, 41
Foila, St................................ 157
Foilan, St.................. See Foellan, St.
Foilenna, St.................. See Foila, St.
Foillan, St..............................60
Forbes' *Kalendar of Scottish Saints* .....
....69
Fore 23, 67
Fore, Abbot of...........................213
Fortchern, St. 128, 217
Forth (River) 100
France 99, 153
Freshford...................See Achadh-Ur
Friesland 137
Froheins 60
Fursæus, St.................. See Fursey, St.
Fursei-domus................. See Froheins
Fursey, St......................59, 60, 77
Galloway 77
Galway 60, 130, 157
Garbh, St. .... See Fanchea, St.
Garbhan, St.............................211
Garthwys, St..................................
...........See Kentigern Mungo, St.
Gaul 60, 133, 169, 188
Gerald, St...............................179
Germanus of Auxerre, St................
...................................151, 188
Gildas the Wise, St. ....
......................75, 171, 224, 225
Gistilian, St. 154
Gistlian, St. .... See Gistilian, St.

Gladys, St...............................217
Glamorgan...............................75
Glamorganshire 149
Glasgow 51, 163
Glastian, St. 83
Glastianus, St.......... See Glastian, St.
Glastonbury Abbey........37, 71, 101
Glastonbury, Abbot of................41
Glenthsen, Abbot of.................147
Gloucester, Bishop of 99
Gloucestershire 130
Gobnata, St..............................114
Gobnet, St. .... See Gobnata, St.
Govan on the Clyde 171
Granard, St. 76
Gregorian Mission 34
Gregory the Dialogist, St. 95, 225
Guagán Barra...........See Lough Erc
Guasacht, St..............................76
Gundleius, St........See Gwynllyw, St.
Gundleus, St........See Gwynllyw, St.
Guthlac, St................................38
Gwen, St. 165
Gwenleue, St........See Gwynllyw, St.
Gwynllwg 75, 217
Gwynllyw Farfog, St......................
.........................See Gwynllyw, St.
Gwynllyw Milwr, St. ....
.........................See Gwynllyw, St.
Gwynllyw, King..........................75
Gwynllyw, St. 217
Gwynnin, St.............. See Vimin, St.
Hampshire 111
Hanbury (Staffordshire)..............97
Headford...................................60
Henry VIII, King.................98, 193
Herbert, St. 199
Herefrith, St..............................147
Hermes, St. .... See Erbin, St.
Hia, St............................ See Ia, St.
Hierlath, St. .... See Jarlath, St.
Hilda, St....................... 107, 113
Historia ecclesiastica gentis Anglorum
.................................95, 113, 225

Holy Well 27, 56, 77, 81, 115
Holywood Monastery.................. 69
Honey Farm............................. 119
Honorius, St. 53
Humber 226
Huna, St. 119
Hy-Many 23
Hywyn, St................................ 33
Í Chaluim Cille.................. *See* Iona
Ia, St...................................... 97
Ibar, St. 185
Ida, St.......................... *See* Ita, St.
Île Lavret............................... 158
Illtyd, St. 33
Inchcleraun 43
Inchebroida Island.................... 36
Indract, St. 101
Inis Breachmhaigh...................... 89
Inis Cathaigh ...... *See* Scattery Island
Iniscarra 169
Inis-coel 85
Inishbofin 130
Inishowen Peninsula 177
Inisquin 60
Inner Farne............................. 198
Inner Hebrides 225
Innerny 152
Innis-Clotran ....*See* Inchcleraun
Inver...................................... 81
Inver Naile 81
Iona..
    55, 79, 86, 109, 123, 127, 129,
    152, 155, 225, 226
Iona, Abbot of ... 141, 154, 173, 203
Ireland ....
    23, 25, 27, 33, 34, 36, 37, 41, 43,
    59, 67, 76, 77, 79, 89, 91, 92, 93,
    95, 103, 108, 115, 120, 123, 128,
    129, 133, 137, 147, 152, 153,
    161, 169, 173, 179, 187, 188,
    189, 195, 201, 205, 207, 211,
    219, 225, 229
Island of Farne......................... 205
Island of Inniscorthy................. 169

Isle of Anglesea....................... 149
Isle of Arran........................... 157
Isle of Bardsey..........................24
Isle of Man..............................79
Isle of May 159
Isle of Thanet 41
Ismael, St. 49
Ita, St. 25, 55, 56, 179
Ives, St. ....*See* Ia, St.
Jarlath, St. 94
Jarrow 47
Jersey....................................65
Jerusalem 37, 110
John of Shanghai and San Francisco,
   St.................................... 231
John the Archcantor....................47
John the Saxon, St.................... 137
Kenen, King..............................65
Kennocha, St. 209
Kennotha, St............ *See* Kevoca, St.
Kent.............................. 41, 141
Kentigern Mungo, St. 50, 163
Kentigern of Glasgow, St.................
   .... *See* Kentigern Mungo, St.
Kentigern, St.............................
   .... *See* Kentigern Mungo, St.
Kentigerna, St........................ 36, 41
Kessog, St............................. 173
Kevin, St. 123
Kevoca, St. 179
Kewe, St. .... *See* Kigwe, St.
Keyna, St.............................. 107
Keynsham 107
Kiara 31
Kiara, St.................................31
Kiara,St.................................31
Kieman, St. .... *See* Kieran, St.
Kieran of Clonmacnoise, St. ....
   .... 43, 162
Kieran, St.................. 161, 162, 217
Kigwe, St................................. 107
Kigwoe, St.................. *See* Kigwe, St.
Kilbarry.............................. 123
Kil-Colgan............................. 157

Kildare 85, 91, 92
Kildare, Abbess of 23, 93
Kileely .... *See* Kil-Faile
Kil-Faile 157
Kilian, St. 89
Kilkeary 31
Kilkenny 34, 120, 195, 205
Kill-Abban Abbey 185
Killane 24
Killeany 201
Killeedy 55, 56
Killega, Abbot of 203
Killeigh 211
Killeshin .... *See* Glenthsen
Kill-Fursa .... *See* Tuam, Diocese of
Killossey, Bishop of 195
Kilmallock 211
Kilmarnock 152
Kinawley 81
Kinawley Church 81
Kinglassie 83
Kinnera, St. .... *See* Cannera, St.
Kinnia, St. 94
Kintyre Peninsula 171
Kontakion of SS. Ethenia and
    Fidelmia 45
Kontakion of St. Brigid of Kildare
    92
Kontakion of St. Cuthbert of
    Lindisfarne 198
Kontakion of St. Ergnad 38
Kontakion of St. Felix of Dunwich
    168
Kontakion of St. Gobnata 115
Kontakion of St. Patrick 188
Kyle, St. .... *See* Kennocha, St.
Kyndeyrn, St. ....
    .... *See* Kentigern Mungo, St.
Kyntire 83
Kyran .... *See* Kieran, St.
Kyran of Clonmacnoise, St. 201
Lactan, St. 195
Lagny 60
Laicin, St. .... *See* Molagga, St.

Laisrén mac Nad Froíc, St. 81
Lake Derwenwater 199
Lake District 50, 199
Lamalisse, St. 157
Landévennec 158
Laoghaire, King 45
Lasar, St. 217
Lassar, St. .... *See* Lasar, St.
Lassera, St. .... *See* Lasar, St.
Lastingham 154
Lastingham, Abbot 153
Laudatus, St. .... *See* Lleudadd, St
Laurence of Canterbury, St. 95
Lawdog, St. 69
Leinster 92, 128, 157, 169, 185
Leitrim 89
Leix 34
Leland 168
Lennox 173
Lérins 47
Letard, St. .... *See* Liudhard, St.
Liath-Mochoemoc 179
Liath-Mochoemoc, Abbot of 179
Libellus responsionum 95
Lichfield 159
Lichfield, Bishop of 154
Liephard, St. 99
Life of St. Brigit 93
Life of St. Finnbarr of Cork 181
Lilleshult 195
Limerick 211
Limerick, Bishop of 25
Lindisfarne 55, 163, 198, 226
Lindisfarne Gospels 163
Lindisfarne, Abbot of 129
Lindisfarne, Bishop of ....
    .... 117, 127, 129, 198
Lindsey, Bishop of 147
Lisbon 92
Lismore 69
Lismore, Bishop of 73
Lismore, St. 109
Little Sodbury 130
Liudhard, St. 99, 141

Llancarfan 75
Llandaff, Diocese of 110
Llanddwyn 77
Llandeilo Fawr 110
Llandybie 87
Llanengan 109
Llanerchymedd 94
Llanlibio 149
Llanmadog 149
Llanrian 168
Lleudadd, St. 56
Llibio, St. 149
Lo of Coutances, St. 56
Loch Lomond 36
Loman, St. 128
London 105, 143, 153
Longford 43, 76, 103
Lough Derg 207
Lough Erc 181
Lough Melvin 90
Lough Ree 103
Louth 92, 94, 147
Lua, St. 195
Lucca 106
Lucius, King St. 23
Luman, St. .... See Loman, St.
Lumiar 92
Macartan, St. 208
Macartin, St. .... See Macartan, St.
Maccarthen, St. ...... See Macartan, St.
Mac-Glastian, St. ..... See Glastian, St.
Mackessog, St. .... See Kessog, St.
Madianus, St. .... See Madoes, St.
Madoc, St. .... See Maidoc, St.
Madoes, St. 90
Máedóc, St. ....
.... See Áedan of Ferns, St.
Maelchu 76
Maelrhys, St. 24
Maghera 207
Magonsæte 139
Maidoc, St. 108, 149, 205
Mainchín mac Setnai, St. ....
.... See Munchin

Mainistir Fhear Maí 67
Malmesbury Abbey 71
Marnan, St. .... See Marnock, St.
Marnanus, St. .... See Marnock, St.
Marnoc, St. .... See Marnock, St.
Marnock, St. 152
Martyr of Canterbury and
    Greenwich 177
Martyrologium Hieronymianum ....
.... 226, 234
Martyrology of Ængus 175
Martyrology of Donegal 85
Martyrology of St. Jerome ....
    See *Martyrologium Hieronymianum*
Mayo 23
Mayo of the Saxons 130
Mayo, Diocese of 179
Meath 128, 219
Meda, St. .... See Ita, St.
Mel of Ardagh, St. 92
Mel, St. 103
Melchno, St. .... See Mel, St.
Melchu, St. .... See Mel, St.
Mellitus, St. 95
Melrose Abbey 198
Melrose Abbey, Prior of 139
Melrose, Abbot of 117
Menevia ....
.... See St. David's Monastery
Mercia 139
Mercia, King of 61
Merewald 61
Merewalh 139
Merewenna, St. 111
Merinus, St. 33
Milburga, St. .... See Milburgh, St.
Milburgh 61
Milburgh, St. 139
Mildburh, St. .... See Milburgh, St.
Mildgyth, St. 61
Mildgytha, St. 139
Mildred, St. 61, 139
Milton Abbey 65
Minster, Abbey of 119

Minster-in-Thanet 61, 139
Mochaemhog, St. ....
.... *See* Mochoemoc, St.
Mochelloc, St. 211
Mochoemoc, St. 179
Mochta, St. 203
Mochua, St. .... *See* Cuan, St.
Modan, St. 100
Modomnock, St. 120
Molagga, St. 67
Mo-Mhaedog, St. .... *See* Maidoc, St.
Monan, St. 152
Moncan, St. .... *See* Cuan, St.
Monmouthshire 107
Motalogus, St. .... *See* Mochelloc, St.
Mottelog, St. .... *See* Mochelloc, St.
Mt. Mairge 34
Mun, St. 103
Munchin, St. 25
Mungo, St. ....
...........*See* Kentigern Mungo, St.
Mura McFeredach, St. 177
Murames, St. ....
...........*See* Mura McFeredach, St.
Muran, St. ....
...........*See* Mura McFeredach, St.
Naile, St. .... *See* Natalis, St.
Naomh Bhríd ....
.... *See* Brigid of Kildare, St.
Natalis, Abbot 169
Natalis, St. 81
Nathalan, St. 38
Nennius, St. 61
Newport 217
Non, St. 157
Nonna, St. .... *See* Non, St.
Nonnita, St. .... *See* Non, St.
Normandy 60
Northamptonshire ....
.... 38, 75, 147, 163
Northumberland 198
Northumbria 55, 70, 153, 227
Oda of Canterbury, St. 149
Odran, St. 131

Offaly 211
Olcan, St. .... *See* Bolcan, St.
On the Ruin and Conquest of Britain ...
See *De Excidio et Conquestu
Britanniæ*
Oncho, St. 108
Onchuo, St. .... *See* Oncho, St.
Orkney Islands, Bishop of 121
Orosius 225
Osburga, St. .... *See* Osburgh, St.
Osburgh, St. 219
Osred, King 195
Ossory 161, 162
Ossory, Bishop of 161, 173
Oswald, St. 149
Oswiu, King 47, 227, 228
Oswy, King 107, 130
Ouil of Normandy, St. 105
Owen, St. 159
Palladius, St. 173, 188
Paris 60
Paschal Controversy ....
...........33, 36, 43, 130, 227, 228
Patrick, St. ....
37, 45, 76, 91, 92, 94, 95, 103,
128, 131, 133, 161, 162, 185,
187, 188, 189, 195, 203, 208,
211, 224
Paulinus, St. 151
Peada of Mercia, King 127
Pega, St. 38
Pelagian Heresy .... *See* Pelagianism
Pelagianism 33, 227
Pembrokeshire 152, 158, 168
Penda of Mercia 77, 163
Peronne 60
Perranporth 162
Perthshire 173
Pestilence of A.D. 664 ....
.... 53, 67, 139
Peter of Canterbury, St. 34
Peterborough Abbey 163
Petroc, St. 75
Picardy 141

Picts.................60, 77, 83, 181, 195
Piran, St. 162
Plain of Gwyddno...................... 149
Portugal...................................... 92
Principium Creaturarum.............. 113
Prosper of Aquitaine.................. 225
Psalter of St. Caimin 207
Puffin Island .... *See* Ynys-Seiriol
Pulcherius, St. ....
.....................*See* Mochoemoc, St.
Pyran, St....................... *See* Piran, St.
Quivoca, St. .... *See* Kevoca, St.
Ramsbury, Bishop of 71
Ramsey............................... 149, 168
Ranus.............................*See* Rhian
Raphoe.. 81
Rathmat...................................... 60
Reculver...................................... 41
Regensburg 37
Rhian 168
Rian ....*See* Rhian
Richard, St. 105, 106
Rioch, St. .... *See* Mel, St.
Ripon.......................193, 198, 205
River Humber.............................. 70
River Shannon........................... 169
Rochester Cathedral.................. 143
Rochester, Bishop of.................... 53
Roman 198
Roman Practice.............................
...........47, 86, 130, 198, 226, 228
Roman, St. 109
Rome ....
33, 38, 43, 47, 99, 101, 106, 110,
169, 181, 226
Romsey, Abbess of...................... 111
Roscommon...............97, 123, 167
Rosneath.................................... 100
Ross, Bishop of 181
Rossory 24
Russian Orthodox Church Outside
Russia.............................. 193
Samson, St. 33, 65, 110
Sawl, St. 57

Saxburgh, St. 119
Saxons............................. 34, 60, 75
Scarthin, St. .... *See* Schotin, St.
Scattery Island 83, 169
Schotin, St. 34
Scotland...
27, 36, 38, 41, 50, 51, 67, 77, 85,
89, 100, 111, 115, 117, 121, 129,
130, 152, 159, 171, 173, 181,
195, 197, 209, 225, 227
Scots 77, 83, 171, 181
Sedna, St................................... 173
Seiriol, St. 94
Seir-Kieran Abbey, Abbot of...... 173
Seithenin 149
Selyf, St. 158
Senames, St.................*See* Senan, St.
Senan, St..................... 83, 169, 207
Senlis, Bishop of........................ 141
Serf, St. 51
Shaftesbury Abbey 193
Sheppey 119
Sherborne, Bishop of 39, 209
Shropshire 195
Sigebert, King St. 60, 77, 127, 168
Sigfrid, St................................... 165
Sillan, St. 150
Silvanus, St. ....*See* Sillan, St.
Silvester, St. 173
Sincheall, St. 211
Sithney...................................... 137
Slebhene, St. 155
Slebhine, St. .... *See* Slebhene, St.
Slieve-Donard 207
Sligo 67, 123
Société des Bollandistes............. 228
Somerset 37
Somersetshire 107, 137
Southern Picts, Bishop of the......*See*
Trumwin, St.
St. Aldate Church (Oxford)...........99
St. David's Monastery................ 154
St. David's, Diocese of......... 69, 151
St. Edward Brotherhood 193

St. Herbert's Island 199
St. Ives (town) 97
St. Kessog's Cairn 173
St. Mogue's Church 89
St. Paul's Cathedral (London) ... 143
St. Vigean..................................... 67
St. Woollos Cathedral 217
Staffordshire 97
Steyning 107
Stirling 100
Stowe... 147
Stowell, T.E.A. 193
Strabo.. 55
Strathclyde 50, 209
Strathclyde, Bishop of................. 51
Suairlech, St. 213
Suffolk................................. 60, 168
Surrey.. 193
Sussex.. 107
Swithun, St. 209
Swords, Abbot of 185
Synod of Brefi 152
Synod of Whitby..............................
    129, 130, 179, 198, 226, 227,
    228
Synod on the Alne 111
Tallacht, Abbot of...................... 175
Talmach, St................................. 181
Tearmann Bearaigh ....
    .... See Termonbarry
Tech Telle 31
Tehelly ....See Tech Telle
Teilan, St....................... See Teio, St.
Teilio, St........................ See Teio, St.
Teilus, St. .... See Teio, St.
Teio, St.. 110
Teiou, St. .... See Teio, St.
Teliou, St. .... See Teio, St.
Termonbarry............................... 123
The Acts of a Wonder-Working Triad
    .... See Colgan, John
The Acts of St. Foila 157
Thelian, St. .... See Teio, St.

Theodore of Canterbury, St. ....
    ....41, 47, 107, 111, 153, 171
Theodoric Paulus...................... 192
Thomian, St................................. 43
Thorgyth, St................................ 78
Thorney 147
Tibba, St. ....
    See Cyneburgh, Cyneswith and
    Tibba, SS.
Tipperary 31, 173, 179
Toimen, St. ....See Thomian, St.
Tola, St. 219
Tortgith, St. ....See Thorgyth, St.
Tregaron 161
Trentham..................................... 97
Trien, St...................................... 203
Trienan, St. ....See Trien, St.
Trim, Bishop of 128
Troparion of St. Brigid of Kildare ...
    91
Troparion of St. Cuthbert of
    Lindisfarne............................ 197
Troparion of St. Edward the Martyr
    192
Troparion of St. Ergnad 38
Troparion of St. Felix of Dunwich
    167
Troparion of St. Gobnata.......... 115
Troparion of St. Patrick............. 187
Trumwin, St................................ 111
Tuam, Diocese of......................... 60
Tudclyd, St................... See Tudy, St.
Tudy, St. 87
Tuscany....................................... 106
Twelve Apostles of Ireland ....
    .... 61, 162
Tybie, St....................... See Tudy, St.
Tydie, St....................... See Tudy, St.
Ulster 24, 81, 93, 133
Ultan, St. 60, 93
Vannes... 75
Ven. Bede ....
    .... See Bede the Venerable, St.
Vimin, St. 69

Voloc, St. 85

Vulcanius, St.....*See* Mochoemoc, St.

Walburga, St. 106

Wales ....
24, 33, 34, 51, 75, 77, 87, 89, 94,
109, 110, 120, 123, 151, 161,
169, 217, 227

Wareham 193

Waterford 55, 73, 89, 115, 211

Wearmouth 47, 165

Weedon 75, 97, 147

Wenedoc, St. ....*See* Enodoch, St.

Wenlock, Abbess of 139

Wenog, St. 27

Werburg, St. 97

Werburgh, St. 98, 119, 147

Wessex 53, 105

Westmeath...................... 59, 67, 213

Westminster 39

Wexford....................................... 89

Whitby Abbey..................................
.... 107, 111, 113, 171, 228

Whitby, Synod of...............................
.... *See* Synod of Whitby

Wilfrid, St.......................................
.... 107, 153, 171, 226, 229

Wilgils, St. 70

William of Worcester 168

Willibald, St. 106

Willibrord, St. 70

Wilson-Claridge, J.E. 193

Winchester 65, 209

Winchester, Diocese of 177

Winebald, St............................... 106

Winwaloe, St. 158

Woking....................................... 193

Wonder-worker 23, 197, 199

Woollos, St. .... *See* Gwynllyw, St.

Woolos the Bearded.........................
.........................*See* Gwynllyw, St.

Woolos the Warrior ....
.........................*See* Gwynllyw, St.

Worcester, Bishop of................. 149

Worshipper of Christ.......................
.... *See* Cele-Christ, St.

Wulfhere (King of Mercia) ....
.... 97, 119

Wulsin, St.....................................39

Wynnin, St. .... *See* Vimin, St.

Ynys-Seiriol 94

York.. 153

York, Archbishop of.......... 149, 171

Yorkshire 168, 213

Ytha, St. .... *See* Ita, St.

23807133R00148

Printed in Great Britain
by Amazon

ESTE ACTION BOOK

PERTENECE A

BRANDING

METHOD

Cómo crear marcas que provocan, venden e impactan

+ 25 HERRAMIENTAS PASO A PASO

Carolina Kairos

Sobre el autor
CAROLINA KAIROS

Me despidieron de la mejor agencia de branding del mundo y al día siguiente creé la mejor agencia para mi mundo: PADAWAN®. Unos meses después tenía beneficios y equipo, siguiendo mi propósito, potenciando a mis clientes y siendo coherente con mis valores. Esto no fue suerte, fue branding.

Conocer estrategia de marca fue clave para lanzar con éxito mi proyecto y tener beneficios. En un entorno hipercompetitivo y en la mentalidad del "todo gratis" hacer las cosas bien ya se da por hecho, no es diferenciador ni aporta algo valioso a tus consumidores. Hay que dar más. Ahora más que nunca solo los más ágiles, certeros y valientes seguirán siendo relevantes.

Por eso, quiero que tú aciertes a la primera y hagas lo que quieras con tu vida. Te comparto de forma práctica mis 8 años en activo en el mundo del branding. Todo lo que he aprendido, todo lo que me ha funcionado y todo lo que he puesto en práctica en más de 100 grandes clientes.

Tienes en tus manos toda la potencia de la estrategia de marca hecha método. Juega con ventaja, provoca, diviértete, marca a fuego, lánzate al mundo. Vive con libertad, crea marcas soberbias.

"Hazlo o no lo hagas, pero no lo intentes."

Yoda

Carolina Kairos es CEO & Head of strategy en Padawan®. Es la creadora de la metodología THE BRANDING METHOD™ y Talent Branding Design™.

Ha trabajado en la gestión de marcas como Carls Jr, Tony Roma´s, Cepsa, Vodafone, Coca-Cola, Museo Thyssen e Iberia entre otras multinacionales. Cada año lanza más de 10 marcas de emprendedores y Startups. Es mentora certificada de estrategia y emprendimiento para programas de entidades como el Banco Santander.

Para más información sobre la autora entra en www.thebrandingmethod.com o www.padawanbranding.com

HAZ LO QUE QUIERAS · HAZ LO QUE QUIERES · QUEMA TUS NAVES

A TI DE MI,

Quema tus naves, ahora.
Como cualquier buen libro de estrategia,
nace en la batalla.

Cuenta la leyenda que esta frase la dijo Alejandro
Magno al empezar la conquista de la costa Fenicia.
Cuando desembarcó, se dio cuenta que su adversario era
mayor que su ejército. Tenía todo en su contra: menos
hombres, menos barcos y menos armas. Pero en vez
de huir, Alejandro mandó quemar sus propios barcos
incendiándolos hasta las cenizas.
Al no tener escapatoria -para poder vivir- solo tenían una
opción: ganar.

Vivimos pensando que tenemos salvavidas, que podemos
retroceder y volver a estar a salvo. Pero la realidad es que
vivimos sin naves. Si quitas de tu mente la posibilidad de
retirada, solo te queda el ahora, el momento y tus actos.

Tu presente es el presagio de tu futuro. Tu vida es lo que
haces con tus días.

Esta es la filosofía con la que trabajo y el propósito de
este libro. No hay plan B, todo lo que no sea conseguir
nuestros objetivos directamente no será.
Pero para hacer lo que queramos, primero debemos saber
qué es lo que queremos.

Bienvenido, ya vemos tierra.

Índice

¿Cómo usar THE BRANDING METHOD? 10
Los 5 DRIVERS 12
¿Para qué sirve el branding? 16

1. THE BRAND EGO · DRIVER 1 · ANÁLISIS DEL CONSUMIDOR

Introducción al driver 26

1. THE DOG MATRIX 28
¿Te estás dirigiendo a la persona correcta?

2. THE FEEL MAP 36
¿Sabes qué necesita realmente?

3. BRAND DESIRE CANVAS 44
¿Qué quiere ser gracias a ti?

4. ATTITUDINAL JOURNEY 52
¿Cómo le haces sentir especial?

5. THE BRAND EGO 60
¿Qué miedo evitas?

2. THE BRAND GANG · DRIVER 2 · FORTALEZA COMPETITIVA

Introducción al driver 76

1. THE MAX PYRAMID 78
¿Tienes lo que hace falta para jugar?

2. THE BRAND TERRITORY 86
¿Qué espacio ocupas?

3. ABC ROLL AXIS 94
¿Elevas o unes?

4. REVOLUTION MATIX 102
¿Contra quién compites?

5. THE 5 FRIENDS 110
Innovación o morir

3. THE BRAND ESSENCE · DRIVER 3 · PLATAFORMA Y ADN DE MARCA

Introducción al driver 124

1. LOS 5 QUÉS DEL BRANDING 130
Si desapareces, ¿importa?

⊛ 2. THE CORE VALUE 138
¿Tu esencia es valiosa?

� 3. BRAND POSITIONING MODEL 144
¿Te creo?

◉ 4. PROPÓSITO 150
¿Puro pose o causa justa?
  + CHECK

◆ 5. BRAND VALUES 158
Eres lo que haces, no lo que dices

⬤ 4. THE BRAND IDENTITY · DRIVER 4 · ASSETS E IDENTIDAD DE MARCA
Introducción al driver 174

◯ 1. THE BRAND SYMBOL 180
¿Qué representas?

🦋 2. CHARISMA ARCHETYPES 188
¿Cómo actúas?

💬 3. TONE OF VOICE PATH 198
¿Cómo comunicas?
+ NAMING + TAGLINE

OO 4. FULL BRAND BOARD 214
¿Cómo evocas?

◻ 5. THE SENSE SQUARE 222
¿Qué sienten?

✳ 5. THE BRAND EXPERIENCE · DRIVER 5 · ACTIVACIÓN DE MARCA
Introducción al driver 236

W 1. WHY WE? 238
¿Por qué tú?

≡ 2. BRAND NARRATIVES 246
¿Qué quieres contar?

↻ 3. BRAND RITUALS.. 254
¿Cómo tangibilizas tu experiencia?

✲ 4. THE 10 GOLDEN MOMENTS 262
Haz que tu cliente siga el viaje

⚇ 5. THE BURN PYRAMID 270
¿Te recordaré mañana?

¿Y AHORA QUÉ?
Unas palabras 280
THE BRAND POWER 282

¿CÓMO USAR
THE BRANDING METHOD?

♫ **¡Escanea y descubre toda la experiencia!**

1

2

3

4

Haz lo que quieras

El libro está dividido en 5 drivers. Cada uno es una etapa clave de creación de marca. Recomiendo seguir este orden pero puedes utilizar cada driver de forma independiente.

Haz lo que quieres

Dentro de cada driver encontrarás 5 herramientas (tools) a activar. Pinta tu libro, garabatea tus ideas, escribe en él sin miedo. Provoca, juega, innova. Para eso está.

Quema tus naves

Cada tool sigue la misma estuctura: **MEET THE TOOL** con la introducción al concepto y su importancia y **PLAY THE TOOL** con la herramienta de Branding Agile lista para poner en práctica.

Repite

Vuelve a THE BRANDING METHOD cada vez que necesites lanzar una marca o producto, poner en marcha un proyecto, replantear tu empresa o lo que quieras.

Comparte tu proceso creativo con la comunidad brander en:

 CAROLINA KAIROS    @LADYBRANDING    @THEBRANDINGMETHOD_BOOK

LOS 5 DRIVERS

5 ÁREAS CLAVE DE TODA ESTRATEGIA DE MARCA

DRIVER 1 · THE BRAND EGO
Análisis del consumidor

Entiende la diferencia entre quién te compra y quién te consume. No podemos hablar igual a todas las personas que se relacionan con nuestra marca. Debemos detectar y mapear bien a los diferentes perfiles decisores para ofrecerles lo que necesitan, realmente. ¿Qué significas para tus clientes y qué necesitan para comprarte? Definirás las acciones para ser relevante, sorprendente y valioso para tus seguidores. Pasa de tener clientes a fans. Tu mejor vendedor es un cliente enamorado.

5 TOOLS PRÁCTICAS A ACTIVAR:
THE DOG MATRIX · THE FEEL MAP · BRAND DESIRE CANVAS · ATTITUDINAL JOURNEY · THE BRAND EGO

DRIVER 2 · THE BRAND GANG
Fortaleza competitiva

¿Por qué deberían volver a comprarte una vez que ya te han probado? ¿Qué te hace ser la mejor opción? ¿Qué competidor está haciendo cosas diferente? ¿Qué sector nuevo te podría hacer competencia? Detecta con estas tools las oportunidades competitivas para capitanear el mercado. Pasa de ser uno más a una elección directa. Juega con ventaja. Abre camino.

5 TOOLS PRÁCTICAS A ACTIVAR:
THE MAX PYRAMID · THE BRAND TERRITORY · ABC ROLL AXIS · REVOLUTION MATRIX · THE 5 FRIENDS

DRIVER 3 · THE BRAND ESSENCE
Plataforma y ADN de marca

Una visión, un propósito. ¿Por qué haces lo que haces? ¿Estás siendo realmente único, diferente y valioso para tus clientes? Define tu esencia, posicionamiento, valores y propósito.
Crea el cuadro de mandos para guiar tu éxito. Define tu camino y tu destino. Haz latir el corazón de tu marca.

5 TOOLS PRÁCTICAS A ACTIVAR:
LOS 5 QUÉS DEL BRANDING · THE CORE VALUE · BRAND POSITIONING MODEL · PURPOSE CHECK · BRAND VALUES

DRIVER 4 · THE BRAND IDENTITY
Assets e identidad de marca

No hay una segunda oportunidad para una primera impresión. Crea todos los activos de tu marca: verbales, sensoriales, simbólicos, actitudinales y visuales. Te reconocerán e identificarán rápidamente. Diseña tu logotipo, los colores corporativos, el estilo fotográfico... pero también la simbología y la experiencia al relacionarnos con ella.
Activa y maximiza todas tus oportunidades. Comunica sin decir ni una sola palabra. Capitaliza todos tus activos y puntos de contacto.

5 TOOLS PRÁCTICAS A ACTIVAR:
THE BRAND SYMBOL · BRAND CHARISMA ARCHETYPES · TONE OF VOICE PATH · FULL BRAND BOARD · THE SENSE SQUARE + NAMING + TAGLINE

DRIVER 5 · THE BRAND EXPERIENCE
Activación y lanzamiento

Crea tu estrategia de lanzamiento y experiencia de marca. Tangibiliza tu promesa. Hazla palpable, que erice la piel. Define tu plan de alianzas de marca para que ganes en repercusión e impacto. Sé el escenario de tus clientes. Ponles buena música. Hazles vivir una gran historia. Cuenta al Mundo que has llegado. Conecta, importa, impacta.

5 TOOLS PRÁCTICAS A ACTIVAR:
WHY WE? · BRAND NARRATIVES · BRAND RITUALS · THE 10 GOLDEN MOMENTS · THE BURN PYRAMID

¿PARA QUÉ *** SIRVE UNA MARCA?

¿CÚANTO MÁS VALE EL AMOR?

¿SOMOS BOBOS LOS CONSUMIDORES?

Piensa en una caja azul turquesa. Piensa en cruasanes. Piensa en amor.

Piensa en Audrey Hepburn desayunando en Nueva York.

¡Brillo y acción!

Seguro que tienes una marca en tu mente ahora mismo, que representa lo que acabo de evocar. Seguramente estés pensando en Tiffany & Co y hasta ahora no había mencionado los diamantes.

Un anillo solitario de Tiffany & Co de 1 quilate, tallado en brillante con una pureza VS2 en platino, cuesta -en marzo de 2022- 13.900 euros. Su equivalente de otra prestigiosa marca como Baunat, es de 8.482,10 euros. Esto es una diferencia de un 61% menos o más, según se mire.

¿Cómo es posible esta diferencia de precio si el anillo es exactamente igual? ¿Cómo es posible que Tiffany & Co siga existiendo si vende "más caro" lo mismo? ¿Somos bobos los consumidores?

Pues, básicamente, porque no vende lo mismo. En materia, puede que los dos sean átomos de carbono brillantes, pero en esencia, significado y valor, Tiffany y Baunat no son semejantes.

Como consumidores posmodernos no solo compramos productos por su funcionalidad. Compramos los significados emocionales y símbolos que contienen sus marcas. Identificarnos para poder diferenciarnos.

Gracias a una sublime gestión de su identidad y su imagen a lo largo de los años, Tiffany, se ha apropiado de significados universales, valiosos y reconocibles, como el amor eterno, la elegancia, el glamour y el cuidado. Baunat para muchas personas no ha significado nada, e incluso es la primera vez que escuchan hablar de esta marca de Amberes.

Una marca es una respuesta emocional ante un elemento funcional. Esto es, que tú asocies e identifiques una piedra pulida y brillante vendida por Tiffany al amor eterno y a la elegancia. Crees en su superioridad y la prefieres, invirtiendo un 61% más en ella. Su marca te aporta un valor emocional frente a la competencia. Y, ¿qué hay más emocional que el amor eterno?

Nuestra misión como branders es crear, comunicar y potenciar todo el valor de nuestra marca, el tangible y racional pero también el intangible y emocional. Alineando nuestra imagen e identidad para que representen lo que buscamos. Generando *awareness*, **elección, recomendación y repetición. Haciendo que nuestra marca capitalice el 100 por 100 de su poder, tangible e intangible.**

Tú decides que marca quieres ser: Baunat con los mejores diamantes del mundo o Tiffany con el mejor valor del mundo.

Eres lo que significas, vales lo que importas.

Entonces, ¿cuánto más vale el amor?

STRATEGY IS POWER

POWER

IS STRATEGY

THE
BRAND
EGO

ANÁLISIS DEL CONSUMIDOR

THE BRAND EGO

"Nolite dare sanctum canibus neque mittatis margaritas vestras ante porcos"

San Mateo

"No des lo sagrado a los perros ni eches perlas a los cerdos, las pisotearán"

SOLO LAS PERSONAS COMPRAN
TODOS TUS CLIENTES SON ALGUIEN

Independientemente del servicio, producto o experiencia que quieras vender, hay una cosa indiscutible que tienen todas las marcas en común: vendes a personas y te compran personas. Por el momento, no hay ninguna inteligencia artificial que necesite nada de lo que puedas ofrecerle.

Todos tus ingresos vendrán de una decisión de compra que tomará alguien. Alguien a quién le aportas valor o no. Que dirá tú o él. Los decisores no son entes abstractos, son personas.

Por eso, es fundamental empatizar y entender las motivaciones de compra de tus clientes. Saber quiénes son, quién quieren ser y qué quieren obtener de ti como marca. Repito, no sirve de nada "echar perlas a los cerdos" ya que no podrían apreciarlas jamás.

Si no sabes quién es tu cliente no puedes llegar a él.
Si no sabes qué quiere realmente de ti, no puedes dárselo.

Al final, todas las transacciones son un beneficio mutuo. Un *win-win*. Todos tus clientes querrán obtener algo de ti, algo que consideren valioso o que les pueda aportar un beneficio a futuro. Vales lo que importas.

Créeme, si no te considerasen valioso o útil no te comprarían. Si tú no quisieras sacar algún beneficio personal de este libro no lo estarías leyendo.

Así funciona el Mundo -repito- vales lo que importas.

DRIVER 1 · 5 TOOLS PARA ANALIZAR A TU CONSUMIDOR Y CLIENTE

1. THE DOG MATRIX
¿HABLAS O LADRAS?

2. THE FEEL MAP
¿SABES QUÉ NECESITA REALMENTE?

3. BRAND DESIRE CANVAS
¿QUÉ QUIERE SER GRACIAS A TI?

4. ATTITUDINAL JOURNEY
¿CÓMO LE HACES SENTIR ESPECIAL?

5. THE BRAND EGO
¿QUÉ MIEDO EVITAS?

BENEFICIOS DE ACTIVAR EL DRIVER 1:

- Mensajes customizados y personalización
- Creación de nichos actitudinales
- Más satisfacción y lealtad
- Humanización de nuestra propuesta
- Capitalización de valores emocionales a través de nuestra marca
- Vinculación emocional y creación de una love brand
- Potenciación y motivación de tu comunidad de marca

THE
DOG
MATRIX

¿HAS PROBADO LA COMIDA PARA PERROS?

¿HABLAS O LADRAS?
QUIEN TE COMPRA NO ES SIEMPRE QUIEN TE QUIERE

¿Qué es?

Supongo que nunca has probado la comida de perros, ¿o sí? Las recenas después de una noche de fiesta pueden dar para mucho. Pero bueno, te preguntarás qué tiene que ver todo esto con innovación y consumidor. Pues mucho, al final es un ejemplo muy fácil para ilustrar nuestra primera herramienta: la diferencia entre cliente, consumidor, cliente ideal y oportunidad perdida.

Esta tool mediante un símil sencillo, te facilita el mapeo de perfiles. Para que puedas diferenciarlos, para que sepas a quién vender tu producto y cómo enfocar tu estrategia de comunicación y marketing.

¿Por qué es importante?

Entender la diferencia entre quien te compra y quien te consume es fundamental. No puedes hablar igual a todas las personas que se relacionan con tu marca. Debes detectar y mapear bien a los diferentes perfiles decisores para ofrecerles lo que necesitan.

Cada perfil clave necesita ciertos motores de compra. No nos importan las mismas cosas ni buscamos los mismos beneficios.

Saber qué mensajes, justificantes y *proof points* tienes que mandar a cada una de las personas que se va a relacionar con tu marca es determinante. Debes comunicar de forma valiosa y acertada. Y por supuesto, en su lenguaje. Entonces... ¿hablas o ladras?

MEET THE TOOL

¿HABLAS O LADRAS?

Para ilustrar la tool, te pongo como ejemplo el caso de una marca de comida premium para perros mini de Londres. Esta marca va a lanzar un anuncio para vender su nuevo pienso. Es sabido que la reina de Inglaterra es una amante de los perros mini, en especial de los de la raza Corgi. La marca, como es lógico, quiere conquistarla y que sea ella una de sus clientas. ¿Quién sería mejor prescriptor y embajador de marca que la propia Elizabeth II? Pero en este caso, el producto se lanza en un supermercado de pueblo a las afueras de Londres, muy lejos de palacios y reyes.

¿A quién nos tenemos que dirigir? ¿Cómo tenemos que contar que nuestra marca es la mejor del Mundo? ¿Ladramos al perro o convencemos de nuestra superioridad al dueño?

Te presento los 4 perfiles clave a mapear en esta tool:

1. THE GUY/ El tipo: Tu cliente es quien compra el paquete de comida, es decir, el dueño del perro.

2. THE DOG / El perro: Tu consumidor es quien va a utilizar el producto o servicio directamente, el beneficiario directo. En este caso el perro.

3. THE QUEEN / La reina: Tu cliente ideal o público objetivo es quien te gustaría que te comprase. En este caso, ¿quién sería mejor comprador que la Reina de Inglaterra amante de los perros mini? ¿Te imaginas una prescriptora como Elizabeth II?

4. THE SNAKE / La cobra: Tu oportunidad perdida es la cobra. Aquel usuario que se interesó por ti pero del que nunca volviste a saber nada. Un doble *check* en leído. ¡Qué te han hecho la cobra, vamos!

Conoce a tus protagonistas y habla su idioma. Identifica a tu tío, tu perro, tu reina y tu cobra para poder saber a quién vendes y quién te compra.

Piensa un momento: Quién toma la decisión de compra, ¿es el mismo que el que paga?

Quién usa tu producto, ¿es el mismo que lo compra?¿Estás dirigiendo tu comunicación de venta al decisor de la compra o al que consumirá el servicio o producto?

¿Por qué se han interesado en ti y, a continuación, te han dejado? ¿Quién ha sido? Entonces... ¿hablas o ladras?

THE DOG MATRIX

MAPEA TUS 4 PERFILES CLAVE

THE GUY

Tu cliente es quien
te compra.
Quien decide gastar su
dinero en ti.

CLIENTE

THE DOG

Tu consumidor es quien te
consume. El que disfruta y
se beneficia directamente
tu producto o servicio.

CONSUMIDOR

THE QUEEN

Tu cliente ideal es
aquella persona o
grupo que sería el
idóneo y a quien
aspiras llegar.

PÚBLICO OBJETIVO

THE SNAKE

Tu oportunidad perdida
es quien se interesó por tu
marca pero que finalmente
se decantó por un
competidor o un producto
sustitutivo.

OPORTUNIDAD PERDIDA

PLAY THE TOOL

THE DOG

CONSUMIDOR

THE GUY

CLIENTE

THE DOG MATRIX

THE SNAKE

OPORTUNIDAD PERDIDA

THE QUEEN

PÚBLICO OBJETIVO

THE
FEEL
MAP

TODO EL MUNDO MIENTE

YO Y MIS CIRCUNSTANCIAS, TODO EL MUNDO MIENTE

EMPATIZA CON TU CLIENTE, ENTIENDE SU SITUACIÓN PERSONAL Y SU ENTORNO. NO TE CREAS NADA DE LO QUE TE DICE.

¿Qué es?

Lo que expresamos no es siempre lo que sentimos. Lo que decimos no es lo que pensamos. Para ser relevante para nuestros clientes debemos entender su contexto, tanto interno como externo.

Entender cómo los factores y elementos externos y la relación con la sociedad afectan a su racionalidad y decisiones internas. Esto es fundamental para poder anticipar sus motivaciones, anhelos, decisiones y necesidades de consumo.

¿Por qué es importante?

Vivimos sobreexpuestos a estímulos, a normas sociales y a estándares impuestos.

Nuestro yo social no es necesariamente nuestro yo real. Por eso, debemos ir más allá de lo que públicamente dice y hace nuestro cliente para poder entender qué siente realmente.

Es importante saber su contexto real. Quién está debajo de la máscara, quién es cuando se quita los zapatos en casa.

Empatiza con él, habla su idioma y ofrécele lo que de verdad necesita, no lo que dice que necesita.

39

MEET THE TOOL

Responderemos las
preguntas de la tool
teniendo en cuenta
las dos dimensiones

FEEL IN VS FEEL OUT

¿Es posible ser 100 por 100 coherente entre lo que se piensa y lo que se hace?

Una vez leí que nuestra vida son nuestros días y, a no ser que seas un maestro zen, es innegable que nuestro entorno exterior condiciona nuestro interior.

Diferenciamos dos grandes dimensiones en esta matriz:

1. FEEL OUT · NUESTRO YO EXTERIOR

Analizamos una dimensión basada en NUESTRO YO EXTERIOR, donde mapeamos y empatizamos con todos los estímulos que recibe de su entorno, cómo actúa e interactúa de cara a los otros. Buscamos encontrar las emociones que experimenta nacidas de los estímulos externos de su realidad cotidiana a los que se expone día a día.

2. FEEL IN · NUESTRO YO INTERIOR

Analizamos una dimensión basada en NUESTRO YO INTERIOR, donde empatizamos con las reflexiones y sentimientos personales de nuestro cliente. Lo que se guarda solo para él: sus pensamientos, anhelos, pasiones y miedos. Los sentimientos nacidos de las emociones.

Es fundamental trabajar las dos dimensiones para empatizar con los sentimientos y acciones de nuestro usuario a mapear.

"LA GENTE NO DICE LO QUE PIENSA NI HACE LO QUE DICE"

THE FEEL MAP

FEEL OUT

PENSAMIENTOS A CORTO PLAZO
PROVENIENTES DE ESTÍMULOS EXTERNOS
PASAJERO
OBSERVADO POR OTROS
RESPUESTAS A ESTÍMULOS EXTERNOS
SOCIAL / PÚBLICO
COTIDIANO
EMOCIONAL

FEEL IN

PENSAMIENTOS A LARGO PLAZO
PROVENIENTES DE EMOCIONES INTERNAS
DURADERO
OBSERVADO POR UN CÍRCULO ÍNTIMO
RESPUESTAS A EMOCIONES INTERNAS
PERSONAL / ÍNTIMO
ASPIRACIONAL
SENTIMENTAL

01
——
¿Qué escucha y ve?

02
——
¿Qué se dice a sí mismo?

03
——
¿Qué opina?

04
——
¿Qué piensa?

05
——
¿Qué hace?

06
——
¿Qué quiere?

FEEL OUT · YO EXTERIOR

PLAY THE TOOL

01

Lo que le rodea, un ambiente de trabajo falso todo, after work lo mismo

—
¿Qué escucha y ve?

03

Que hay que hacer lo mismo para estar a la altura.

—
¿Qué opina?

05

Comportarse como el resto para ser aceptado.

—
¿Qué hace?

FEEL IN · YO INTERIOR

02

Tengo ganas que sean las 5.
piensa como cualquiere, al final no somos
muy diferentes, todos cagamos, follamos, etc

___
¿Qué se dice a sí mismo?

04

Piensa en el tiempo eibre suen
de ese ambiente forzado.

___
¿Qué piensa?

06

Quiero lo mismo que todos,
llegar a casa y quitar la
careta, comer pizza, tirar
pedas tranquilamente, relajarse.

___
¿Qué quiere?

si pienso lo que quiere igual tengo que enfocar
más hacia ese yo en zapatiella.

BRAND
DESIRE
CANVAS

¿PARA QUÉ SIRVE UN ZAPATO?

SUELAS ROJAS Y FLORES AZULES

Si piensas que un zapato solo sirve para proteger tus pies al caminar estarás de acuerdo en que solo debes tener un par en tu armario.

Estoy segura que eso no es así, y eso, se lo debemos al consumo simbólico. ¡Bienvenido al fin del consumo utilitario o puramente funcional!

Un zapato -o mejor dicho, el logo estampado en él, su suela roja o su forma icónica- nos representa. No dice lo mismo usar unos zapatos de marca Vans que unos Balenciaga.

Sí, los dos sirven para caminar, pero el que los compra no busca exponer y evocar lo mismo a través de ellos. Tampoco valen lo mismo, ¿no?

Seguramente alguien con Vans quiere expresar rebeldía y ser vinculado a un entorno informal, mientras que alguien con unos zapatos de suela roja como los que diseña Christian Louboutin busca expresar estatus y poder adquisitivo. Quien compra unos zapatos Balenciaga no paga exclusivamente por su amortiguación.

¿Qué es?

Somos consumidores simbólicos. El consumidor postmoderno -osea tú y yo- construye su identidad como individuo a través de la utilización de símbolos. Valores aceptados por diferentes grupos sociales que permiten al individuo posicionarse y expresarse. Haciendo suyos ciertos valores asociados a las marcas (estatus, rebeldía, tradición...)

Por lo tanto, los objetos y sus marcas son percibidos como contenedores de valor. Nos aportan significado como individuos y nos ayudan a desarrollar un papel en la sociedad. Mediante las marcas afirmamos y construimos nuestro *self* o identidad.

Por eso, la funcionalidad del producto ya no es el único *driver* de compra y, ni mucho menos, el más importante.

¿Por qué es importante?

Para entender las motivaciones de tu cliente en los diferentes prismas de su vida. Lo que piensa de sí mismo, pero también lo que quiere que su entorno social piense de él al utilizar tu marca.

Hemos pasado del utilitarismo a las motivaciones, pura personificación de marca. Vivimos en la era de la fragmentación, el consumidor crea su identidad mediante diferentes objetos de consumo.

MEET THE TOOL ───────────

FARDAR ES AMAR

Además de analizar lo que el consumidor piensa de tu marca como tal, es importante que analices lo que él piensa de sí mismo y su entorno al utilizar tu marca.

Qué estás significando para él y qué quiere transmitir a los demás al poseerte o utilizarte.

ANALIZAMOS LOS 4 DESEOS:

SELF
¿Qué piensa de sí mismo al poseer tu marca? ¿Qué autoimagen tiene de sí mismo al utilizarte?

ENEMY
¿Qué pensaría si un competidor suyo poseé tu marca y él no? ¿Se sentiría amenazado, envidioso, tranquilo, triste...?

FRIEND
¿Qué pensaría de un amigo suyo que utiliza tu marca? ¿Tendría ganas de imitarle?

SOCIAL
¿Qué quiere que sus amigos/ entorno piensen de él al comprar tu marca? ¿Qué estatus o rol social quiere ejercer gracias a ti?

   >>Volvamos al ejemplo de la marca de comida para perros premium para ejemplificar la tool.

BRAND DESIRE CANVAS

SELF
AUTOIMAGEN O SEGURIDAD

¿Qué piensa de sí mismo cuando compra tu marca?

SOY UN BUEN DUEÑO

ENEMY
DOMINIO O PODER

¿Qué pensaría si un competidor suyo tiene tu marca y él no?

TIENE DINERO PARA COMPRAR PIENSO PREMIUM PODER ADQUISITIVO

FRIEND
ASPIRACIONES

¿Qué pensaría si un amigo suyo comprase tu marca?

QUIERO QUE MI MASCOTA LA PRUEBE

SOCIAL
ESTATUS - ROL SOCIAL

¿Qué quiere que sus amigos piensen de él al comprar tu marca?

CUIDA A SU PERRO Y SE PREOCUPA POR DARLE SOLO LO MEJOR. NO ESCATIMA EN GASTOS. LE VA MUY BIEN. ES CUIDADOSO Y DETALLISTA

PLAY THE TOOL

SELF
AUTOIMAGEN O SEGURIDAD

¿Qué piensa de sí mismo cuando compra tu marca?

Que invierte en calidad, comodidad, Tranquilidad, salud y status.

FRIEND
ASPIRACIONES

¿Qué pensaría si un amigo suyo comprase tu marca?

yo también quiero probar.

ENEMY
DOMINIO O PODER

¿Qué pensaría si un competidor suyo tiene tu marca y él no?

Haría lo posible por tenerle también.

SOCIAL
ESTATUS - ROL SOCIAL

¿Qué quiere que sus amigos piensen de él al comprar tu marca?

Que se cuida, que vive bien que tiene suerte.

BRAND DESIRE CANVAS

ATTITUDINAL
JOURNEY

ERES COMO COMPRAS

¿QUÉ TIENEN TODOS LOS EXCÉNTRICOS EN COMÚN?

Seguramente conoces a alguien que acamparía en la puerta de una tienda para hacerse con el último modelo de un teléfono. Pero también conocemos a alguien que sigue sin utilizar Whatsapp. ¿Sabes qué tienen en común estos dos perfiles extremistas? Pues, llamar la atención.

Cómo consumimos dice mucho de nostros. Con esta tool detectarás y mapearás las 5 actitudes que existen. Comprender para vender. Juega a su juego.

¿Qué es?

Los consumidores somos prismáticos. Si es cierto que para ciertos servicios o productos realizamos compras impulsivas, para otros necesitamos pruebas y mucha meditación para saber si nuestra decisión es acertada o no.

Podemos estipular que existen 5 tipologías de patrones de comportamiento frente al consumo, en relación con la aceptación de lo que consideramos novedoso o a lo que no estamos acostumbrados.

Las he bautizado como las 5 actitudes de consumo y se dan siempre independientemente del sector o producto:

1.EL DEVOTO: Voto, consagración, dedicación total a una experiencia o marca.

2.EL VISIONARIO: Se anticipa a su tiempo previendo hechos o inaugurando algo.

3.EL PRAGMÁTICO: Necesita de la práctica, la ejecución o la realización de las acciones y no de la teoría para pasar a la acción y confiar.

4.EL CONSERVADOR: Es favorable a la continuidad de sus formas de vida actuales. Es reticente al cambio.

5.EL ESCÉPTICO: Duda o desconfía de la verdadera eficacia o posibilidades de algo, especialmente de las creencias comúnmente aceptadas.

¿Por qué es importante?

Imagínalos como un trineo de perros huskies donde los devotos y visionarios tirarán y guiarán de los rezagados y perezosos hacia ti.

Mapea qué actitud está expresando el mercado hacía tu marca. Debes saber qué necesita para confiar y comprar tu producto. Qué le tienes que dar a cada uno y cómo conquistarles para fidelizarles. No te conformes solamente con seducir a un tipo de consumidor, haz que todos se entreguen a la experiencia de tu marca y te adoren.

MEET THE TOOL ───────

Activa las tres etapas:

>>Volvamos al ejemplo de la marca de comida para perros premium para ejemplificar la tool.

1. PROOF POINTS
¿Qué pruebas necesita para confiar en ti?

Al lanzar tu marca te toparás con diferentes perfiles de clientes, y estos necesitarán diferentes pruebas para poder confiar en ti y comprarte.

Habrá perfiles que solo con leer reseñas caigan rendidos a tus encantos y otros auditarán hasta la última coma. Entiende qué necesita emocional y racionalmente para creerte y desearte.

2. FEEL POINTS
¿Cómo le haces sentir único y especial?

Es importante que le mimes y le dediques antención. Una compra es una relación de confianza. Hazle sentir bien. Haz que no se arrepienta de haberte elegido. Haz que farde de consumirte.

¿Qué personaje actúa en el plató de tu marca? ¿Qué sentimientos despiertas en ellos?¿Qué buscan sentir gracias a ti? ¿Por qué te buscan? ¿Por qué te quieren? ¿Cómo activas sus emociones?

3. SWEET POINTS
¿Cómo tangibilizas su experiencia?

A todos nos gusta un buen caramelo. ¿Cómo haces que tus clientes se sientan parte de tu espectáculo? ¿Qué les das para que puedan cumplir su papel de devoto o de escéptico? ¿Qué momentos dulces les haces sentir? ¿Qué acciones tangibles o intangibles activan tu promesa?

Pasa de palabras a hechos. De ideas buenas a dulces caramelos.

+ EMOCIONAL

DEVOTO

VISIONARIO

PRAGMÁTICO

CONSERVADOR

ESCÉPTICO

+ FUNCIONAL

ATTITUDINAL JOURNEY

ACTITUD	PROOF POINTS	FEEL POINTS	SWEET POINTS
Su relación con el consumo y las marcas	¿Qué necesita para estar interesado y confiar en ti?	¿Cómo le haces sentir único y especial?	¿Cómo tangibilizas su experiencia?
Voto, consagración, dedicación y entrega total a una experiencia			
Se anticipa a su tiempo previendo hechos o inaugurando algo			
Necesita la práctica y la ejecución de las acciones. No solo la teoría o especulación	UN AMIGO SUYO LE HA HABLADO DE LA COMIDA. APARECE LA MARCA RECOMENDADA EN BLOGS DE MASCOTAS DE REFERENCIA	LE CUENTAS CURIOSIDADES DE SU RAZA DE PERRO. TE POSICIONAS COMO UN AMANTE DE SU MASCOTA	EL DÍA DEL CUMPLEAÑOS DEL PERRO SE ENVÍA A CASA UNA TARJETA DE FELICITACIÓN CON CUMPLEAÑOS FELIZ LADRADO
Es favorable a la continuidad de las formas de vida actuales			
Duda y desconfía de lo comúnmente aceptado y su eficacia			

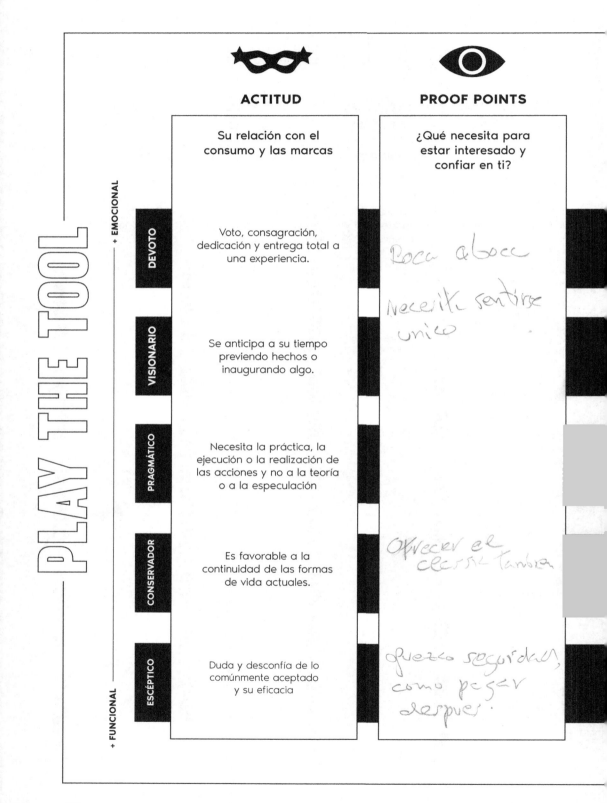

PLAY THE TOOL

ACTITUD

PROOF POINTS

Su relación con el consumo y las marcas

¿Qué necesita para estar interesado y confiar en ti?

+ EMOCIONAL

DEVOTO

Voto, consagración, dedicación y entrega total a una experiencia.

Poca aloce

Necerit sentirse unico

VISIONARIO

Se anticipa a su tiempo previendo hechos o inaugurando algo.

PRAGMÁTICO

Necesita la práctica, la ejecución o la realización de las acciones y no a la teoría o a la especulación

CONSERVADOR

Es favorable a la continuidad de las formas de vida actuales.

Ofrecer el clessic tambra

ESCÉPTICO

Duda y desconfía de lo comúnmente aceptado y su eficacia

guezco segurdad, como pegar despues.

+ FUNCIONAL

FEEL POINTS

SWEET POINTS

¿Cómo le haces sentir
único y especial?

¿Cómo tangibilizas su
experiencia?

Contemplándole,
mandarle
follow up.

Haciéndole sentir
importánte
y privilegiado
por ser mi
cliente
y
poder presumir
de ello

des cuento
historias
de cosas que
aprendo y puede
que le puede
ayudar

Le mando
una felicitación
de cumpleños,

muestras de
cosas que hago
"me acordé de
Ti"

DEVOTO

VISIONARIO

PRAGMÁTICO

CONSERVADOR

ESCÉPTICO

ATTITUDINAL JOURNEY

THE
BRAND
EGO

SÉ EL PARACAÍDAS DE TUS CLIENTES

EL CONSUMIDOR ES EGOÍSTA. TODO LO QUE COMPRA LO HACE POR SU PROPIO BIENESTAR Y BENEFICIO, CONSCIENTE O INCONSCIENTEMENTE.

¿Qué es?

Todo lo que hacemos es un paracaídas, compramos para reducir, minimizar y evitar nuestros miedos y temores.

Como creadores de marcas debemos impactar y vender al inconsciente de nuestros clientes, entendiendo y sabiendo qué miedo o "dolor" evitamos gracias a nuestros productos o servicios.

Hablamos de beneficios pero también debemos pensar en ser un paracaídas. ¿Qué hace tu marca para mejorar la supervivencia y bienestar de tu cliente ?

Si sabemos qué quiere ser nuestro cliente, sabremos ofrecerle lo que cree que necesita. Pero si conocemos qué teme ser o qué evita seremos su aliado y guardián de por vida.

¿Por qué es importante?

Con esta tool descubrirás y definirás las dos motivaciones de consumo de tu cliente: la consciente y la inconsciente.

Sé claro y habla directamente a la seguridad emocional de tus consumidores. Para nuestro cerebro más primitivo evitar el dolor es mucho más importante que obtener placer.

MEET THE TOOL

DOS REALIDADES, DOS MOTIVACIONES

1. SOCIALMENTE CONSCIENTE - APORTA PLACER

En esta dimensión vendemos al cerebro más racional de nuestros consumidores. Pensamos en los beneficios que obtienen gracias a nuestra marca.

Obtendremos y analizaremos respuestas más lógicas, analíticas y estratégicas.

Como por ejemplo "compro buena comida para perros para que mi perro esté más sano".

2. EGOÍSTAMENTE INCONSCIENTE - EVITA EL DOLOR

En esta dimensión venderemos al cerebro más primitivo e instintivo: el reptil. Aquel que nos "mantiene vivos y a salvo". Este que activa respuestas rápidas frente amenazas, sensaciones y emociones personales.

Obtendremos y analizaremos respuestas más instintivas, basadas en la supervivencia y bienestar egoísta.

Como por ejemplo "compro buena comida para perros para que mi perro no se muera y no me quede solo".

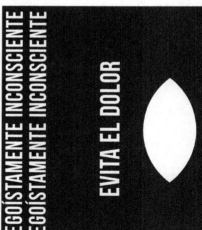

>> Un ejemplo sencillo:
Volvemos a la marca de comida para perros. Esta es premium y el coste es superior a la competencia, pero los valores nutricionales compensan la elección y el coste... ¿no?

THE BRAND EGO

SELF INTEREST	PAIN	GAIN	MEANING
¿Qué beneficios futuros obtiene al utilizar tu marca? ¿Por qué su vida va a ser mejor?	¿Qué le solucionas?	¿Qué elementos valorados socialmente gana?	¿Qué cree que eres para él?
SOY UN BUEN DUEÑO, DOY LO MEJOR A MI PERRO	MI PERRO SE ALIMENTA DE FORMA EQUILIBRADA	MI PERRO ESTÁ MÁS SANO Y FUERTE	SALUD CANINA
¿Qué le hace sentir en este preciso momento?	¿Qué miedo evitas que afecte directamente a su supervivencia física y emocional?	¿Qué tiene que pasar para que no se produzca el temor?	¿Qué eres realmente para él?
MI PERRO ESTÁ CONTENTO, ME QUIERE MÁS, VIVIRÁ MÁS TIEMPO A MI LADO	NO QUIERO QUE MUERA / NO QUIERO QUEDARME SIN SU COMPAÑÍA Y AMOR / NO QUIERO QUEDARME SOLO	UN PERRO SANO VIVE MÁS TIEMPO, GANAS MÁS TIEMPO PARA ESTAR JUNTOS	COMPAÑÍA / SOLEDAD

PLAY THE TOOL

SELF INTEREST

PAIN

SOCIALMENTE CONSCIENTE
APORTA PLACER

¿Qué beneficios futuros obtiene al utilizar tu marca? ¿Por qué su vida va a ser mejor?

¿Qué le solucionas?

EGOÍSTAMENTE INCONSCIENTE
EVITA DOLOR

¿Qué le hace sentir en este preciso momento?

¿Qué miedo evitas que afecte directamente a su supervivencia física y emocional?

GAIN

MEANING

¿Qué elementos valorados socialmente gana?

¿Qué cree que eres para él?

SOCIALMENTE CONSCIENTE
Beneficio racional

¿Qué tiene que pasar para que no se produzca el temor?

¿Qué eres realmente para él?

EGOÍSTAMENTE INCONSCIENTE
Beneficio emocional

THE BRAND EGO

AHORA QUE HAS
ACTIVADO LAS 5
TOOLS DEL DRIVER 1
RESPONDE A CADA
PREGUNTA CON UNA
PALABRA:

¿Qué
obtienen al
comparte?

¿Qué miedos
minimizan?

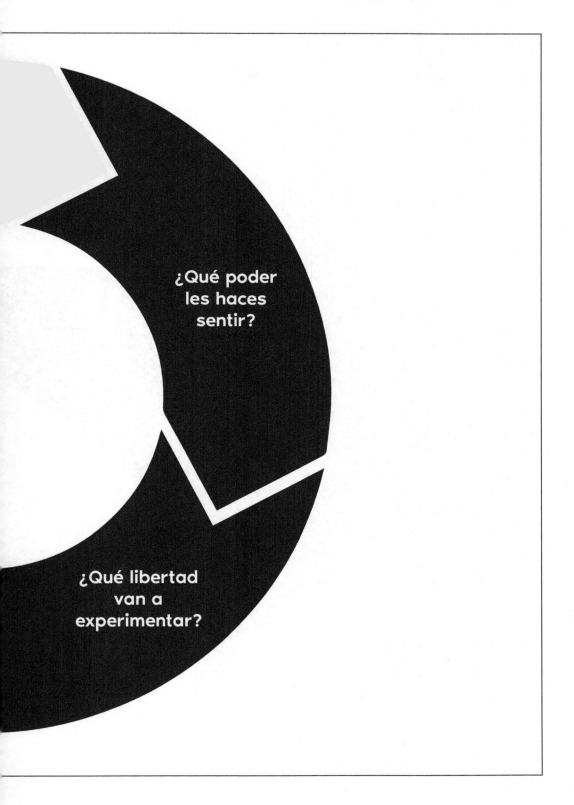

¿Qué poder
les haces
sentir?

¿Qué libertad
van a
experimentar?

DRIVER 2

THE
BRAND
GANG

FORTALEZA COMPETITIVA

DRIVER 2 · FORTALEZA COMPETITIVA
THE BRAND GANG

"At the end, your're different or you're cheaper"

Guy Kawasaki

"Al final, eres diferente o eres barato"

TU COMPETENCIA TE REPRESENTA

Tu competencia no es tu enemigo. Es tu ecosistema, tu banda, tu gang.

Ellos abrieron el camino y gracias a su trayectoria y apredizajes, tú puedes evolucionar y mejorar.

Antes de lanzar cualquier marca, campaña o innovación de producto es importante analizar tu entorno. Tener claro con quién compites y entender perfectamente qué hacen y cómo lo hacen. Analizar es vital para poder definir tu estrategia y posicionamiento.

Estas 5 herramientas te harán tomar mejores decisiones, te darán una foto más completa de cómo está tu ecosistema y qué rol puedes ocupar en él.

¿Por qué no partir de las fortalezas de tus competidores y jugar con ventaja?

Tanto si tu marca ya está en el juego de los negocios como si vas a lanzar una nueva, este driver es fundamental. Todos competimos contra alguien.

Recuerda, tu competencia te representa. Dime contra quién compites y te diré quién eres.

Ponte cómodo, ¡empieza el safari!

DRIVER 2 · 5 TOOLS PARA ACTIVAR TU FORTALEZA COMPETITIVA

1. MAX PYRAMID
¿TIENES LO QUE HACE FALTA PARA JUGAR?

2. THE BRAND TERRITORY
¿QUÉ ESPACIO OCUPAS?

3. ABC ROLL AXIS
¿ELEVAS O UNES?

4. REVOLUTION MATRIX
¿CONTRA QUIÉN COMPITES REALMENTE?

5. THE 5 FRIENDS
INNOVACIÓN O MORIR

BENEFICIOS DE ACTIVAR EL DRIVER:
- Identificar oportunidades y tendencias
- Construir valor desde nuestras fortalezas e innovar
- Saber qué elementos clave tenemos que comunicar
- Crear un territorio competitivo propio
- Liderar y construir una nueva categoría
- Diferenciar la marca con coherencia y competitividad

MAX
PYRAMID

HACER LAS * COSAS BIEN SE DA POR HECHO

TODO CAMBIA PARA QUE NADA CAMBIE

SI TU MAYOR DIFERENCIADOR ES LA INNOVACIÓN ES QUE TE FALTA MUCHA INNOVACIÓN

¿Qué es?

Lo que valoraban tus clientes hace unos años no tiene por qué ser lo mismo que valoren hoy. En un entorno altamente competitivo hacer las cosas bien ya se da por hecho. Que tu producto sea bueno, bonito y llegue rápido, ya no es llamativo ni un diferenciador para ser competitivo. Si no cumples esto, directamente ya no venderás.

Antes de 2020 nadie valoraría la presencia de gel hidroalcohólico o las pantallas de seguridad en un Uber. Antes de Uber no se valoraba la geolocalización de tu conductor. Ahora es fundamental y necesario. Si no la tuviera, la app no sería competitiva, es más, sería contraproducente y le haría perder clientes.

¿Por qué es importante?

Los mínimos de la industria, son la base de la pirámide de la competitividad. Lo básico sin lo cual no podrías estar en el negocio o hacer negocios.

Por ejemplo, si tu valor diferencial es la innovación es que te falta mucha innovación.

Entiende qué es lo básico que compartís todos los competidores. Mapea qué es lo que hace a los referentes ser competitivos y analiza qué hace que el líder domine el mercado.

Examina a tu competencia para partir de una posición ventajosa. Entiende qué es valorado por tu consumidor para poder innovar y ofrecerle algo diferente. Algo único que sea relevante e irresistible. ¡Ah!, y que solo lo puedan conseguir gracias a ti.

MEET THE TOOL

MAX PYRAMID

Existen 3 escalas de atributos que tu marca debe mapear, fortalecer y comunicar

1. ATRIBUTOS HIGIÉNICOS:

Son aquellos sin los que no podrías competir en tu sector. Aquellos servicios, productos o acciones que si no cumples te harán estar fuera del mercado. Mapea y detecta qué es todo lo que tus competidores y tú compartís. Es importante identificarlos para no basar nuestra comunicación exclusivamente en estos atributos pero debemos tenerlos en mente y no olvidarlos.

¿Sin qué mínimos no podrías competir?

2. ATRIBUTOS DIFERENCIALES:

Estos atributos son aquellos que no forman parte de la naturaleza del producto, pero constituyen un valor añadido importante a la hora de su comercialización. Aquellos atributos que comparten los líderes. Que son valorados por tus clientes y que potencian la elección de sus marcas.

¿Qué valora el mercado hoy en día?

3. ATRIBUTOS SINGULARES:

Lo que hace único, diferente y especial. Aquellos elementos inimitables y genuinos que solo se pueden obtener/vivir gracias a su marca.

¿Qué cosas únicas aporta el competidor líder que no pueda imitar ningún otro?

✖ >>Ilustremos la tool con un restaurante mexicano

THE MAX PYRAMID

ATRIBUTOS
SINGULARES

¿Qué
aporta
el competidor
líder que no
tenga
ningún otro?

*EJ: SU SALSA SECRETA,
COMO TE SALUDAN LOS
EMPLEADOS AL ENTRAR*

INNOVA

ATRIBUTOS
DIFERENCIALES

¿Qué tienen en común los
referentes del sector?

*EJ: UN PACKAGING LLAMATIVO Y
DIFERENTE, CONTENIDO DIVERTIDO
EN RRSS, LOCAL ICÓNICO...*

MEJORA

ATRIBUTOS
HIGIÉNICOS

¿Sin qué no serías competitivo?
¿Qué es lo mínimo para estar en el mercado?

*EJ: QUE TUS PEDIDOS LLEGUEN A TIEMPO, QUE LA
CALIDAD SEA BUENA, CUMPLIR LAS NORMATIVAS,
TENER WEB...*

REFUERZA

PLAY THE TOOL

ATRIBUTOS
SINGULARES

¿Qué aporta el competidor líder que no tenga ningún otro?

ATRIBUTOS
DIFERENCIALES

¿Qué tienen en común los referentes del sector?

ATRIBUTOS
HIGIÉNICOS

¿Sin qué no serías competitivo?
¿Qué es lo mínimo para estar en el mercado?

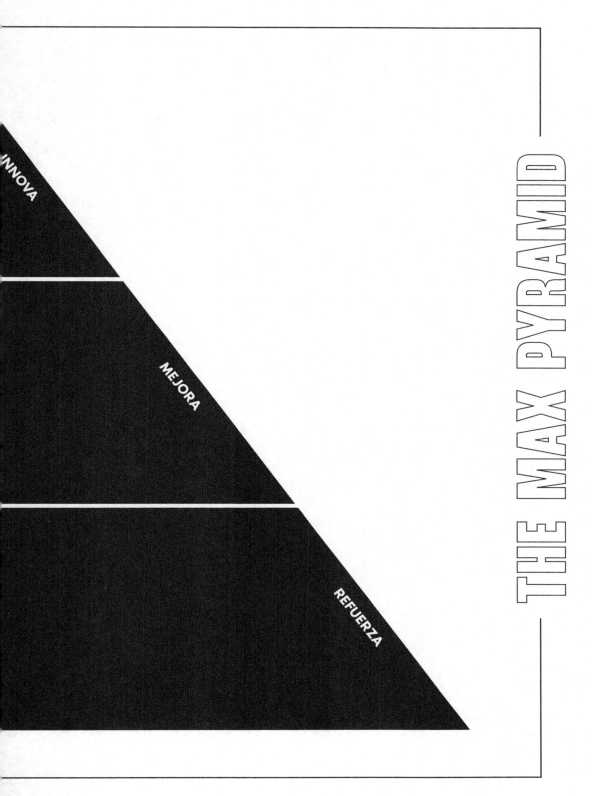

THE MAX PYRAMID

THE
BRAND
TERRITORY

¿CÓMO SUENA TU MÚSICA?

¿CÓMO SUENA TU MÚSICA?
HAZ QUE TUS AUDIENCIAS TE IDENTIFIQUEN RÁPIDO

¿Qué es?

Llamamos territorio de marca al espacio conceptual desde el que competir. Por ejemplo si hablamos de música, hacer comprender de forma rápida a tu oyente que eres un grupo de pop o de rock. Es fundamental que te ubiquen y se hagan una imagen mental rápida, conocida y cotidiana de quién eres y a qué banda perteneces. Luego, ya les tocarás lo que quieras.

Un mismo producto puede tener diferentes territorios de marca en función de su marca. Pensemos en marcas de cervezas. El producto en sí es un *commodity* -zumo de cebada- pero las marcas que lo venden no.

Cuando pensamos en Coronita o Estrella Damm nos viene a la cabeza una imagen muy clara: tomar una cerveza en vacaciones, en la playa, al sol con amigos en un ambiente social festivo diurno.

En cambio, cuando pensamos en Heineken, nos aparece una imagen mental mucho más masculina, nocturna. De pub y deportes.

El producto es siempre el mismo, el territorio de marca no.

¿Es magia? No, es branding.

¿Por qué es importante?

El territorio es la base y cimiento de la marca. Recuerda que una marca es la respuesta emocional a un elemento funcional, como puede ser la imagen o nombre de una compañía, producto o persona.

Como especialistas en branding somos expertos en crear y gestionar percepciones positivas nacidas de nuestro territorio. Comunicar y activar. Serlo, pero también parecerlo. Debemos alinear nuestra identidad -lo que somos- con nuestra imagen -lo que parecemos-.

Nuestro territorio competitivo es ese gran concepto de donde partimos para generar *awareness,* elección, recomendación y repetición. Examina a la competencia para partir de una posición ventajosa. Entiende qué es valorado por el consumidor para poder innovar y ofrecer algo diferente y único que sea relevante para él.

MEET THE TOOL

THE BRAND TERRITORY:
DE LO RACIONAL A LO EMOCIONAL

Existen diferentes formas de segmentar territorios pero, una buena, es mapeando las principales categorías de propuestas de valor. Analizando si nuestros competidores ofrecen propuestas emocionales o racionales.

¿Qué es?

Segmentamos 5 territorios clave:

PRODUCT ORIENTED: Aquellos competidores que basan su propuesta de valor en los beneficios funcionales y racionales de sus productos y servicios. Por ejemplo: el utilitarismo, la innovación, la calidad... Las características propias del servicio o producto en sí.

BRAND ORIENTED: Se centran en sí mismos. Comunican legado, tradición, liderazgo... Basan su propuesta en su propia experiencia y relevancia como sujeto. Ellos mismos como marca son su propio aval.

CUSTOMER ORIENTED: Marcas que comunican los beneficios directos que experimentarás como consumidor al utilizarlas o comprarlas. Por ejemplo: seguridad, placer, belleza, reconocimiento...

SOCIAL ORIENTED: Marcas que buscan un beneficio para toda la sociedad y no solo para sus consumidores. Incitan mediante su uso o consumo a hacer un bien mayor o que sus consumidores dejen de hacer algo "mal".

MEANING ORIENTED: Buscan transcender, cambiar las normas. Que el consumidor y la sociedad se transforme. Marcas que buscan dejar un legado inmaterial, transcendente y valioso. Transforman a su categoría y elevan la exigencia del mercado.

¿Por qué es importante?

Este primer mapeo de territorios ayuda a saber que espacio ocupa nuestra competencia. Qué oportunidades hay. Qué características aún están sin explorar y por qué.

THE BRAND TERRITORY

WHY WE?

PRODUCT ORIENTED	BRAND ORIENTED	CUSTOMER ORIENTED	SOCIAL ORIENTED	MEANING ORIENTED
BENEFICIOS, CALIDAD, PRODUCCIÓN, CAPACIDAD, SEGURIDAD.	LIDERAZGO, TRADICIÓN, HERENCIA, INNOVACIÓN.	SATISFACCIÓN, PLACER, ASPIRACIONES, RECONOCIMIENTO.	RESPONSABILIDAD, CONCIENCIA, COMPROMISO, CONEXIÓN.	TRANSFORMACIÓN, LEGADO, TRANSCENDENCIA, VALOR.
ZARA	**HERMES**	**DESIGUAL**	**TOMS**	**PATAGONIA**
RTG Secret S.	Sense Pamper 2 Urban	Pamper Glo Urban		Glo?

+ RACIONAL —— **+ EMOCIONAL**

PLAY THE TOOL

PRODUCT ORIENTED

BRAND ORIENTED

BENEFICIOS, CALIDAD, PRODUCCIÓN, CAPACIDAD, SEGURIDAD.

LIDERAZGO, TRADICIÓN, HERENCIA, INNOVACIÓN.

+ RACIONAL

CUSTOMER ORIENTED

SOCIAL ORIENTED

MEANING ORIENTED

SATISFACCIÓN, PLACER, ASPIRACIONES, RECONOCIMIENTO.

RESPONSABILIDAD, CONCIENCIA, COMPROMISO, CONEXIÓN.

TRANSFORMACIÓN, LEGADO, TRANSCENDENCIA, VALOR.

THE BRAND TERRITORY

—————————————————— **+ EMOCIONAL**

ABC
ROLL
AXIS

¿POR QUÉ COMPRAMOS COOOOOO OOOOOOOOOO OOOOOOOO OOSAS?

CERCA O LEJOS. TÚ O YO
LLÉVAME AL CIELO DE LO SOCIAL

¿Qué es?

Existen muchos ejes de posicionamiento y en cada proyecto en función de lo que se busque se creará uno nuevo. Pero analizando y sintetizando qué tienen todas las marcas en común identificamos dos ejes que comparten todas. Basados en 4 variables que siempre se repiten independientemente del precio de los productos o servicios, de modas o de las preferencias particulares de sus consumidores.

¿Por qué es importante?

Con este axis podemos entender nuestro rol hacia nuestro consumidor y qué busca lograr a través de nuestra marca.

Es muy útil visualizar donde se está posicionando nuestra competencia para poder tomar decisiones en base a oportunidades o tendencias detectadas. Analizar patrones y obtener una visión más completa de nuestro entorno competitivo, para ocupar un espacio inexplorado o consolidar nuestra propuesta.

MEET THE TOOL ───────────────

DOS EJES, UNA RELACIÓN

CONSUMER ROLL - ALEJAR O ACERCAR - ASPIRACIONAL O DEMOCRÁTICO

El primer eje es la posición que quieren adquirir nuestros clientes ante sus semejantes.

Consumimos productos y experiencias en base a dos factores: lo que nos eleva, posiciona y aleja de los otros y lo que nos acerca a ellos.

El lujo nos aleja de muchos para acercarnos a pocos. La democratización en el consumo iguala, mezcla y une. Estos dos opuestos posicionan a nuestra competencia y a nosotros mismos en torno a estas variables. ¿Qué buscan nuestros clientes a través de nuestra marca? Sentirse como un individuo único y especial o acercarse a la sociedad, a lo democrático, a la tendencia y a la masa.

BRAND ROLL - PASIVIDAD O ACTIVIDAD - FACILITADOR O INSPIRACIONAL

El segundo eje es la proactividad de las marcas hacia sus consumidores.

Existen dos tipos de roles en las marcas:

1. Aquellas que ofrecen soluciones "listas para consumir", donde el consumidor tiene un rol pasivo, beneficiario de las mismas.

2. Aquellas marcas que empoderan a su consumidor para que él mismo, de forma activa, pueda lograr sus objetivos gracias a la marca.

El consumidor debe tomar un rol activo o pasivo frente a tu marca. ¿Le facilitas o le incitas?

Por ejemplo Nike, te empodera para que tú saques la mejor versión de ti mismo inspirándote. En cambio, Decatlhón te facilita todo el material deportivo a buen precio.

ABC ROLL AXIS

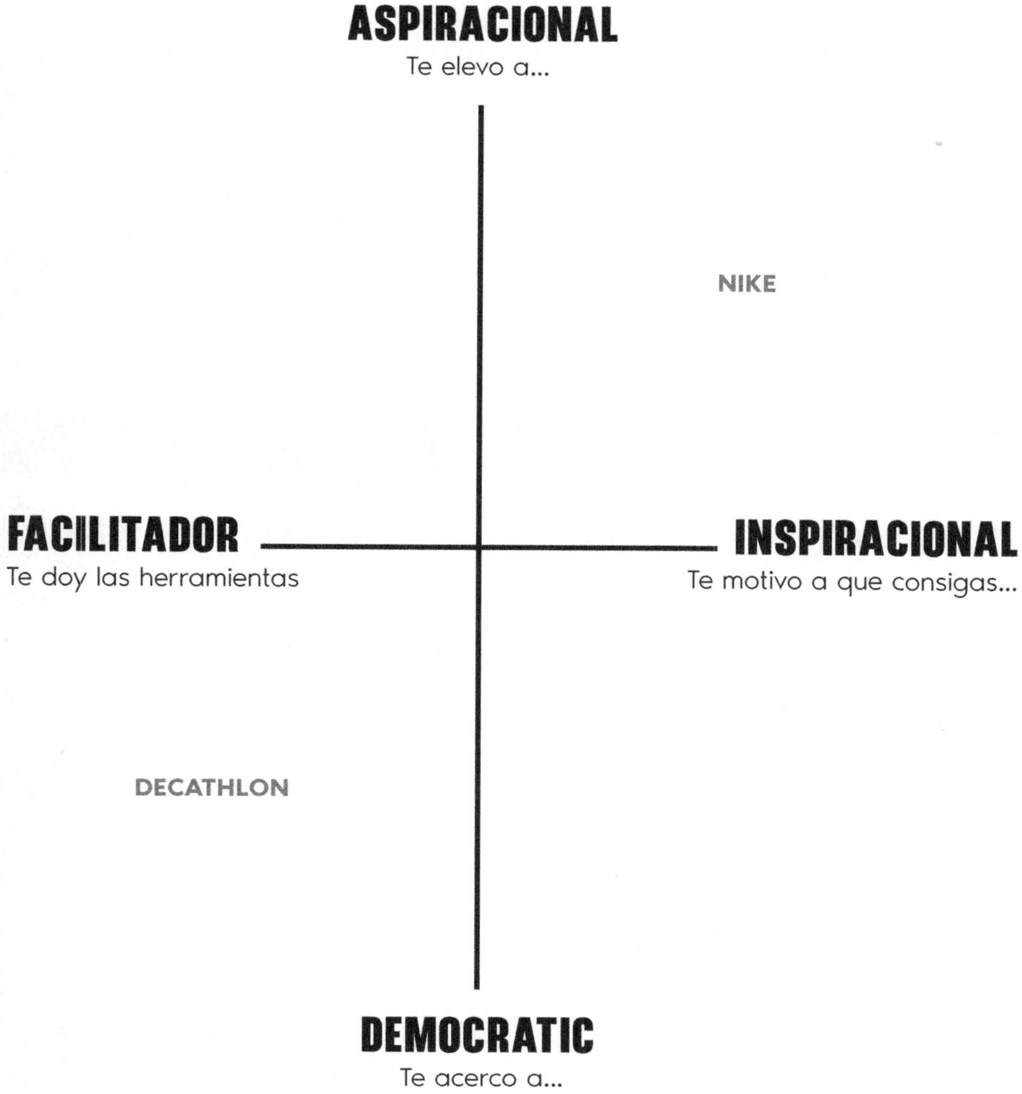

ASPIRACIONAL
Te elevo a...

NIKE

FACILITADOR ──────────── **INSPIRACIONAL**
Te doy las herramientas   Te motivo a que consigas...

DECATHLON

DEMOCRATIC
Te acerco a...

PLAY THE TOOL

FACILITADOR
Te doy las herramientas

DEMOCRATIC
Te acerco a...

ASPIRACIONAL

Te elevo a...

INSPIRACIONAL

Te motivo a que consigas...

ABC ROLL AXIS

REVOLUTION
MATRIX

COMPITES POR MI TIEMPO Y ATENCIÓN
COMPITES POR MI TIEMPO Y ATENCIÓN
COMPITES POR MI TIEMPO Y ATENCIÓN
COMPITES POR MI TIEMPO Y ATENCIÓN
COMPITES POR MI TIEMPO Y ATENCIÓN
COMPITES POR MI TIEMPO Y ATENCIÓN
COMPITES POR MI TIEMPO Y ATENCIÓN
COMPITES POR MI TIEMPO Y ATENCIÓN

CAPITANEA UNA NUEVA CATEGORÍA, CREA LO AÚN DESCONOCIDO
REVOLUCIONA Y REESCRIBE EL SIGNIFICADO DE TU SECTOR. SÉ TÚ QUIEN LIDERE EL MAÑANA

¿Qué es?

En los negocios quien permanece más en el juego es quien gana. Como en la evolución, los animales más resistentes son los que mejor han sabido adaptarse a las necesidades del entorno.

Debemos mirar a los más transgresores, a aquellos que están redefiniendo los significados del sector, pero sin quitar ojo a los líderes históricos, los más resistentes.

De todos, podemos obtener grandes aprendizajes. ¡Pero cuidado! No todos nuestros competidores "venden" lo mismo que nosotros o tienen nuestra misma "forma".

¿Por qué es importante?

Aprende de los más resistentes e inspírate de los innovadores. Pero estate alerta de los revolucionarios que en un primer momento no identificaste como competencia. En ellos está la clave de un cambio de mentalidad y oportunidad.

¿FITBIT ES COMPETIDOR DE TESLA?

Sí, absolutamente. Los dos compiten en el sector de la movilidad. Los dos compiten por el tiempo que sus usuarios pasan con ellos. Mientras conduces un Tesla no puedes andar y mientras mides tus pasos andando con tu Fitbit no puedes conducir un Tesla.

Competimos por la atención y tiempo de nuestros clientes. Todos los segundos de interés o de utilización que empleen en alguien que no seas tú, son tu competencia. Un competidor no siempre es una marca que venda exactamente lo mismo que tú o que tenga tu "misma forma".

Abre la mente y mapea tus oportunidades competitivas. En esta tool analizamos tres tipologías de competencia y competidores. De los 3 tenemos grandes lecciones que aprender y grandes oportunidades que implementar.

MEET THE TOOL

TRES TIPOLOGÍAS DE COMPETIDORES:

1. COMPETIDORES HISTÓRICOS:

Aquellos más resilientes, que más han aguantado jugando en tu sector, aquellas marcas con más *senority*. Por ejemplo, si seguimos en el sector de la movilidad, algunas marcas serían Mercedes, Ford o Porsche. De este gran grupo de competidores debemos preguntarnos: ¿qué les ha hecho mantenerse al frente y seguir siendo relevantes en un entorno cada vez más cambiante y competitivo?

2. COMPETIDORES ESTRELLA:

Aquellos que lideran hoy en día, que son referentes de innovación y transgresión. Los favoritos y los más de moda hoy. Aquellas marcas que han evolucionado aportando mejoras significativas, dando un paso más allá. Las reglas del juego sectorial han cambiado.

Por ejemplo: Tesla y sus coches automáticos eléctricos, los coches compartidos en las ciudades como Zity o Uber. Es importante que en este grupo nos preguntemos: ¿qué han cambiado? ¿Qué han mejorado?

3. COMPETIDORES REVOLUCIONARIOS:

Aquí debemos poner un ojo fuera de nuestra competencia directa y ordinaria e ir más allá. Busca otras empresas complementarias, no necesariamente "iguales que tú" que te han quitado cuota de mercado. Aquellas marcas que han entrado en el juego de forma inesperada y han cambiado los hábitos de nuestros consumidores.

Competir por el uso de productos tiene solución pero una vez que tus consumidores hayan cambiado un hábito de consumo o significado será mucho más complicado seducirles de nuevo. Por ejemplo, Fitbit invita conducir menos y andar más. Esta marca aunque no vende coches compite en movilidad. Por eso, es importante analizar este grupo y plantearse lo siguiente: ¿qué cambio de hábitos han creado en tu cliente? ¿Qué revoluciones ha vivido que hará que ya no de ni un paso atrás? ¿Qué creencias han transformado?

Todo cambia para que nada cambie

Aprende de los más resistentes e inspírate de los innovadores. Pero estate alerta de los revolucionarios que en un primer momento no mapeaste como competidores. En ellos está la clave de un cambio de mentalidad y oportunidad.

REVOLUTION MATRIX

MASTER
HISTÓRICOS

ROCKET
ESTRELLA

RADICAL
REVOLUCIÓN

¿QUÉ COMPETIDORES SON LOS LÍDERES HISTÓRICOS?	¿QUIÉN ESTÁ HACIENDO LAS COSAS DE FORMA DIFERENTE?	¿QUIÉN HA CAMBIADO LAS REGLAS DEL JUEGO?
FORD	*TESLA*	*FITBIT*

¿QUÉ LES MANTIENE ALLÍ?	¿QUÉ LES FUNCIONA?	¿QUÉ INNOVACIÓN LIDERA? ¿QUÉ HA TRANSFORMADO?
VALUE FOR MONEY Y SEGURIDAD	*NUEVO ESTATUS* *ECO = INNOVADOR*	*NO CONDUCIR*

PLAY THE TOOL

RADICAL

REVOLUCIÓN

¿QUIÉN HA CAMBIADO LAS REGLAS DEL JUEGO?

ROCKET

ESTRELLA

¿QUIÉN ESTÁ HACIENDO LAS COSAS DE FORMA DIFERENTE?

MASTER

HISTÓRICOS

¿QUÉ COMPETIDORES SON LOS LÍDERES HISTÓRICOS?

¿QUÉ INNOVACIÓN LIDERA? ¿QUÉ HA TRANSFORMADO?

¿QUÉ LES FUNCIONA?

¿QUÉ LES MANTIENE ALLÍ?

REVOLUTION MATRIX

THE 5
FRIENDS

INNOVACIÓN O MORIR ABRE LA MENTE

OÍD LO QUE LOS DEMÁS NO DICEN
LA INNOVACIÓN TRANSCIENDE A TU SECTOR. MIRA MÁS ALLÁ PARA BUSCAR PATRONES Y ELEMENTOS DISRUPTIVOS. RECUERDA: COMPITES POR MI TIEMPO Y ATENCIÓN

¿Qué es?

Identificar los puntos que tienen en común referentes de tu sector y marcas externas te hará abrir la mente y ver oportunidades que se pueden extrapolar a tu industria.

La innovación y lo que los consumidores valoran de ella es transversal a todas las marcas. Entender qué hace que tus competidores estén en el juego hará que encuentres oportunidades competitivas interesantes.

En esta herramienta te invito a que la mires desde tu propia experiencia como consumidor y pienses en las marcas con las que tú te relacionas, que admiras y las que te inspiran como persona no como brander o trabajador de una empresa o sector.

¿Por qué es importante?

Al alejarnos de nuestro día a día y analizar otros sectores podemos conectar ideas interesantes que, inmersos en nuestro propio sector, no habríamos visto. Es como no ver el bosque por mirar solo los árboles.

La frase "Vanguardia o morir" la vi en las servilletas de Diverxo, el templo de Dabiz Muñoz, y desde entonces, no me he quitado esta afirmación de la cabeza.

Es un excelente ejemplo de cómo otros sectores son inspiración y mejor práctica de innovación fuera de tu *core*. ¿Puede una *brander* aprender branding de un chef?

Sí, siempre.

Innovación o morir

La innovación es subjetiva, para cada uno de nosotros significa
una cosa. ¿Qué significa para ti ser innovador?

¿QUÉ 5 COSAS TIENEN EN COMÚN?

5 MARCAS QUE ESTÉN HACIENDO LAS COSAS BIEN

5 MARCAS INNOVADORAS

5 MARCAS QUE TE INSPIREN

5 MARCAS QUE ESTÉN TRIUNFANDO

THE 5 FRIENDS

Ahora que has activado las 5 tools del segundo driver responde de forma rápida:

INNOVAR ES:

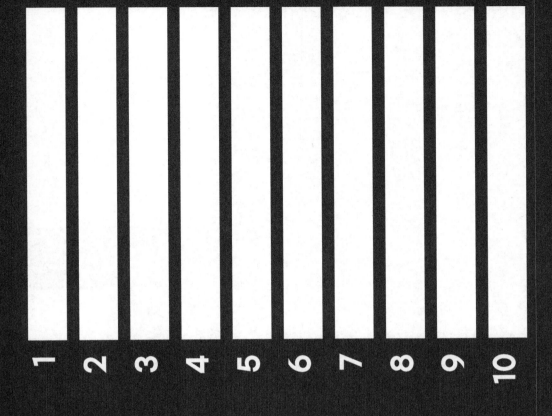

1   2   3   4   5   6   7   8   9   10

**10 oportunidades
e ideas locas que
puedo hacer con
mi marca:**

THE
BRAND
ESSENCE

PLATAFORMA DE MARCA

DRIVER 3 · PLATAFORMA DE MARCA
THE BRAND ESSENCE

"Ignoranti, quem portum petat, nullus suus ventus est"

Lucio Anneo Séneca

"Ningún viento es favorable para el que no sabe a qué puerto va"

TU CAMINO Y TU DESTINO
LA ESENCIA DE TODO: TU MARCA

Nuestra esencia define lo que somos y por qué somos lo que somos. Es el ADN de la marca y su cuadro de mandos.
Todo lo que hacemos, cómo, y por qué lo hacemos, debe partir de nuestra esencia.

Definirla de forma clara, hará que tomemos decisiones desde la estrategia y no desde la táctica o la improvisación. Nos hará seguir un rumbo concreto y habrá un porqué en todas las acciones que hagamos.

Tener una esencia de marca definida, hará que pilotes mejor tu presente. Fijando el rumbo hacia tus objetivos de forma estratégica.

La esencia de marca debe ser lo suficiente flexible para navegar por ella de forma ágil adaptándonos a los cambios. Pero lo suficientemente definida y concreta para no perder el rumbo.

Como dice la frase del filósofo Séneca: "Para un marinero sin rumbo todos los vientos son desfavorables". Recuerda, la esencia es nuestro timón y mapa. Nuestro camino y nuestro destino. El corazón de la marca.

NUESTRA MARCA ES NUESTRO NEGOCIO

La marca navega a favor de nuestro beneficio empresarial. Todas las decisiones y acciones que hagamos deben partir de ella para potenciar e impulsar nuestra competitividad.

Para construir nuestra esencia trabajaremos las 6 dimensiones que coexisten y brotan en todas las marcas. Lo llamo THE BRAND FLOWER

En este driver profundizaremos en el corazón de nuestra marca. Como ya hemos visto, nuestro territorio parte de nuestra competencia y como veremos en el próximo driver nuestra personalidad se activará con nuestra experiencia.

Para hacer lo que queramos, primero tenemos que saber qué es lo que queremos. Y tú ¿quién eres?

THE BRAND FLOWER:
LAS 6 DIMENSIONES
DE LAS MARCAS

6. PERSONALIDAD:

Nuestra actitud hacia el Mundo.
Nuestro carácter e identidad.
Cómo nos comportamos
para que nos perciban como
queremos ser percibidos.

PERSONALIDAD

5. VALORES DE MARCA:

Los principios que nos
mueven. En qué creemos.
Aquellas convicciones
e ideales que guían la
forma en la que nos
expresamos, actuamos y
nos comportamos.

VALORES

4. PROPÓSITO:

Cómo vamos a
impactar en la
vida de nuestras
audiencias. Nuestro
compromiso con el
Mundo.

PROPÓSITO

TERRITORIO

1. TERRITORIO DE MARCA:

Es el espacio conceptual desde
el que competir. El territorio, es
el punto de partida, desde el que
nace la idea de marca. Creando y
capitaneando un espacio propio
para afrontar y liderar el mercado.

CORE

2. CORE:

La luz que nos guía.
Nuestro faro. Nuestro
mantra. El camino y la
base que nos permite
seguir nuestro territorio y
dirección competitiva.

POSICIONAMIENTO

3. POSICIONAMIENTO:

Lo que nos diferencia del resto. Nos
da forma y define lo que somos.
Nos ayuda a responder quién
somos, qué hacemos y por qué
somos importantes para ti.

DRIVER 3 · 5 TOOLS PARA CREAR TU ESENCIA Y ADN DE MARCA

1. LOS 5 QUÉ'S DEL BRANDING
SI DESAPARECES, ¿IMPORTA?

2. THE CORE VALUE
¿QUÉ ME APORTAS?

3. POSICIONAMIENTO
¿TE CREO?

4. PROPÓSITO
¿PURO POSE O CAUSA JUSTA?

5. BRAND VALUES
LO QUE HACES, NO LO QUE DICES

BENEFICIOS DE ACTIVAR EL DRIVER:

- Claridad y rumbo competitivo
- Alineación de toda la organización
- Creación de una propuesta de valor clara y potente
- Diferenciación e identificación
- Comunicación más clara y coherente
- Compromiso con objetivos estratégicos y perdurables
- Experiencia de marca completa y consensuada

129

LOS 5
QUÉ'S
DEL BRANDING

SI ✕

DEJASES ✕

DE ✕

EXISTIR, ✕

¿TE ✕

ECHARÍAMOS ✕

DE ✕

MENOS? ✕

UNA MARCA ES LA RESPUESTA EMOCIONAL A UN ELEMENTO FUNCIONAL

SERLO, PERO TAMBIÉN PARECERLO

¿Qué es?

Crear una marca competitiva además de atractiva es nuestra misión como especialistas en branding.

Para ello, nuestra marca debe responder y cumplir estos 5 *musts*:

1. SER PERSONAL: debe basarse en una única esencia, algo que la represente y construya desde lo que es, de forma clara.

2. SER AUTÉNTICA: ha de ser creíble de acuerdo a su promesa.

3. SER RELEVANTE: la esencia de la marca debe ser deseable y vital.

4. SER PERDURABLE: la esencia de la marca permanecerá en el tiempo más allá de modas.

5. SER ÚNICA: una marca fuerte es diferente a su competencia, vive su propio territorio competitivo.

¿Por qué es importante?

Tienes 0,4 segundos para enamorar a un posible cliente. En menos de un segundo decide si se queda contigo o no. No eres la última Coca-Cola del desierto. Hay más peces nadando en este mar.

Por eso, debes tener muy clara tu propuesta, tu territorio y dirección competitiva. Saber y expresar de forma clara por qué estás en el juego y por qué eres su mejor opción.

Si no aportas, te aparta.

MEET THE TOOL

CONSTRUYE VALOR DESDE LO QUE ERES

Los 5 qués del branding complementan y responden a los 5 *musts* de las marcas. Usa estas preguntas para mapear y potenciar tu valor competitivo. Responde de forma clara y haz saber al Mundo por qué estás en el mercado y para qué.

LOS 5 QUÉ'S DEL BRANDING:

1. ¿QUÉ EVANGELIZAS?

Aquello que predicas y promueves como propio. Lo que buscas dar a conocer a través de tu marca.

2. ¿QUÉ DEFIENDES?

Aquello que prometes. Lo que buscas cambiar o mejorar gracias a tu marca.

3. ¿QUÉ MOTIVAS?

Aquellos cambios positivos y personales que viven tus clientes gracias al consumo de tu marca. Cómo les haces ser mejor en su día a día.

4. ¿QUÉ ELEVAS?

Aquellos cambios que transcienden a tus consumidores y afectan a todo el entorno. Lo que transformas del Mundo en el que actúas.

5. ¿QUÉ APORTAS?

Aquella mejora valiosa frente a lo ya existente. Más allá de ser uno más, lo que te hace diferente ante tus competidores.

LOS 5 QUÉ'S DEL BRANDING

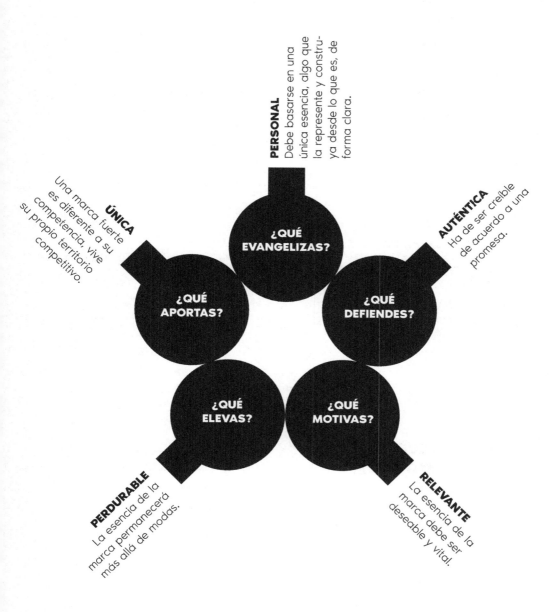

PERSONAL
Debe basarse en una única esencia, algo que la represente y construya desde lo que es, de forma clara.

ÚNICA
Una marca fuerte es diferente a su competencia, vive su propio territorio competitivo.

AUTÉNTICA
Ha de ser creíble de acuerdo a una promesa.

¿QUÉ EVANGELIZAS?

¿QUÉ APORTAS?

¿QUÉ DEFIENDES?

¿QUÉ ELEVAS?

¿QUÉ MOTIVAS?

PERDURABLE
La esencia de la marca permanecerá más allá de modas.

RELEVANTE
La esencia de la marca debe ser deseable y vital.

Como ves, cada pregunta parte de un principio.
Ahora responde a cada una con una sola palabra.

PLAY THE TOOL

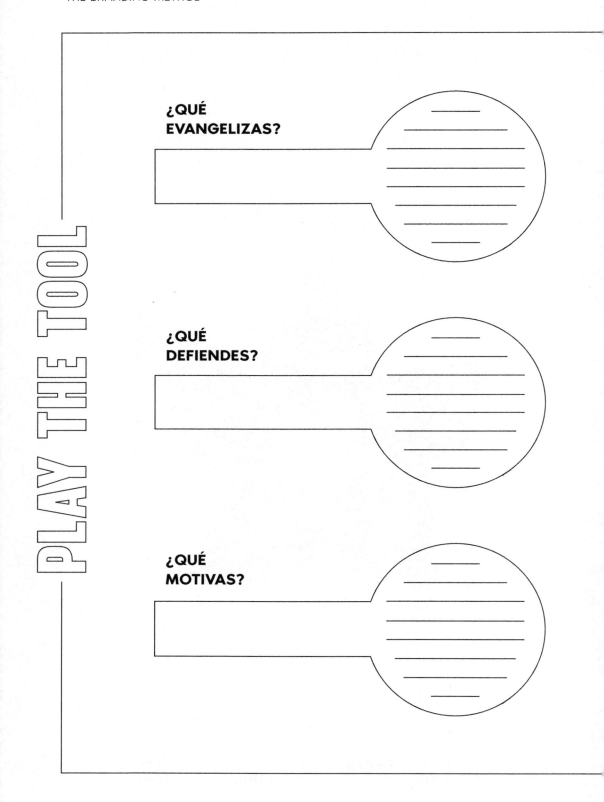

¿QUÉ EVANGELIZAS?

¿QUÉ DEFIENDES?

¿QUÉ MOTIVAS?

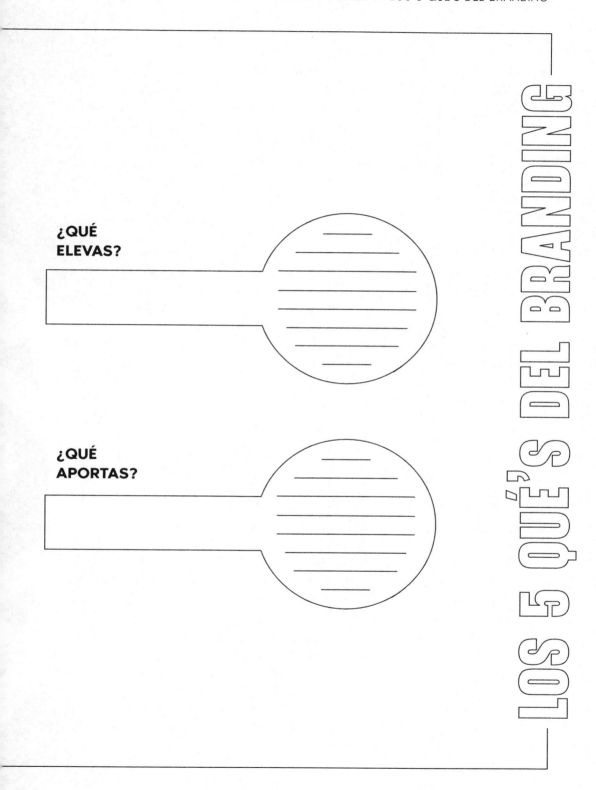

¿QUÉ ELEVAS?

¿QUÉ APORTAS?

LOS 5 QUÉ'S DEL BRANDING

THE
CORE
VALUE

"Si no puedes explicarlo de forma sencilla es que no lo has entendido bien".

A. Einstein

NUESTRO CAMINO Y NUESTRO DESTINO

NUESTRO CORE VALUE ES EL CORAZÓN DE NUESTRA MARCA. ES EL FARO QUE NOS ILUMINA. EL DESTINO, PERO A LA VEZ EL CAMINO A SEGUIR. NUESTRO MANTRA.

¿Qué es?

La síntesis y elixir de nuestra marca. La concreción máxima de por qué existimos, expresado de forma fácil y atractiva.

Define de forma consensuada y clara qué es lo que ofrecemos realmente a nuestros clientes. Sin florituras, solo el valor real y auténtico de lo que somos y la razón por la cual estamos en el negocio.

¿Por qué es importante?

Debemos tener muy claro nuestro objetivo y dirección competitiva, para así materializar nuestra esencia de forma sencilla. Habla claro a tus clientes, escribe como hablas.

Siguiendo este *flow* de 5 preguntas llegaremos a sintetizar al máximo nuestra marca. Tener una propuesta clara es fundamental.

Tu cliente no tiene tiempo de andar descifrando tu marca.

Sé claro. Tenlo claro.

MEET THE TOOL :
PLAY THE TOOL

Time is money, attention is power

Recuerda: "Si no puedes explicarlo de forma sencilla es que no lo has entendido bien".
Tu cliente no tiene tiempo de andar descifrando tu marca. Sé claro. Tenlo claro.

1 ¿Qué quiere obtener tu cliente gracias a ti? _____

2 De verdad, ¿qué quiere realmente gracias a ti? _____

3 Exprésalo de tal manera que lo entienda
una abuela y su nieta pequeña a la vez _____

4 Resúmelo en 3 palabras _____

5 Resúmelo en una palabra y dáselo _____

¿QUÉ ESPACIO QUIERES OCUPAR EN LA MENTE DE TUS CLIENTES?

1. Cuando piensen en _____

2. Cuando quieran _____

3. Cuando vean _____

THE CORE VALUE

_____ quiero que piensen en mi.

_____ quiero que piensen en mi.

_____ quiero que piensen en mi.

BRAND
POSITIONING
MODEL

O TE P*SICIONAS
O TE POSICI*NAN

LO QUE NOS DIFERENCIA DEL RESTO Y NOS HACE ÚNICOS

¿Y TÚ QUIÉN ERES? ¿CÓMO LO HACES? ¿PARÁ QUÉ?

¿Qué es?

El posicionamiento de marca nos da forma. Define lo que somos frente a los otros. Expone de forma clara nuestra propuesta pero también nuestro valor diferencial. Nos ayuda a responder quiénes somos, qué hacemos y por qué somos importantes para nuestros clientes.

¿Por qué es importante?

Entender nuestra posición dentro del conjunto del mercado nos hace poder competir con más claridad. Hace que nuestros clientes puedan apropiarse de elementos valiosos para ellos y saber qué beneficios emocionales y funcionales obtendrán al consumirnos.

MEET THE TOOL : ⸺
BRAND POSITIONING MODEL

Define tu posicionamiento de forma valiosa

Al contar al mundo que has llegado debes impactar pero también convencer. Utilizamos una estructura sencilla que combina elementos racionales con partes más emocionales para buscar un equilibrio convincente y competitivo.

¿QUÉ?

Nuestra promesa hacia el Mundo. Lo que van a vivir gracias a nosotros y por qué somos su mejor opción.

¿CÓMO?

Debemos exponer todos nuestros avales. Nuestra forma de hacer posible lo que prometemos.

¿POR QUÉ?

Además de obtener beneficios económicos, exponer por qué existimos y qué vamos a aportar a lo ya existente.

PLAY THE TOOL

Somos _____

Creemos en _____

Hacemos que las personas puedan _____

_____

Gracias a _____

construimos y transformamos _____

_____

_____

para que el Mundo sea _____

_____

_____

_____

PROPÓSITO
CHECK

¿PROPÓSITO O PURO POSE?

CAPITANEA EL PRESENTE PARA ESCRIBIR EL FUTURO

¿CÓMO VAMOS A IMPACTAR EN LA VIDA DE NUESTROS CLIENTES? ¿CUÁL VA A SER NUESTRO LEGADO Y COMPROMISO HACIA EL MUNDO?

¿Qué es?

El propósito es nuestro compromiso con el Mundo, con el mercado y con nosotros mismos. Buscamos impactar de forma competitiva pero también positiva para todos.

Las marcas no son entes aislados, y, cada vez, tienen más peso en la sociedad y en los acontecimientos sociales. Una marca debe tener claro quién es para saber qué promueve y abandera. Qué causas justas defenderá llegado el momento.

Pero no solo basta decirlo, hay que hacerlo. Un propósito sin una causa justa, es como un *storytelling* sin un *storydoing*, puro cuento.

¿Por qué es importante?

Empoderar, dar las herramientas, facilitar... Entender nuestra marca y nuestro proyecto empresarial como un escalón hacia el bien común. ¿Por qué no además de un beneficio económico buscar una mejora transversal? Coherente tanto para nuestros clientes como para toda la sociedad

Una marca para el Mundo

Debes aspirar a que tu marca sea reconocida como referente y ejemplo de buen hacer. Haz que promueva valores inspiradores y que tus consumidores se sientan orgullosos de ella. Pasa de *"just do it"* a *"do it good for all"*.

"La fórmula de la humanidad dice que debemos tratar a la humanidad siempre como un fin y nunca como un mero medio"

Kant

MEET THE TOOL ————————————

Los 10 mandamientos de una marca con propósito

1. Pasa de Just do it a do it good for all

Busca generar un impacto positivo en tu ecosistema más allá de solo en tus clientes.

2. Busca beneficios más allá de ingresos

Además de obtener un rendimiento económico con tu actividad, ¿por qué no buscar un progreso social, ambiental o educativo? Haz que tu marca y las personas que la conforman mejoren su vida.

3. Crea marcas para personas no solo para consumidores

Empatiza con tu cliente más allá de verlo como una pura transacción económica. Busca ofrecerle un beneficio genuino. Hacer negocios debe ser un *win-win* para las dos partes.

4. Haz marcas que vivan en este Mundo

O te posicionas o te posicionan. Sé una marca que toma partido y tiene un rol activo en la sociedad.

5. Sé coherente además de sostenible

Doing Good is doing good business. Tener propósito no es solo ser ecologista.

PROPÓSITO CHECK

6. Defiende causas justas

Busca aquellas causas con las que empatices y te representen. Tener un impacto positivo empieza en casa.

7. Trasciende en todos los puntos de contacto

Tu propósito lo puedes expresar a través de tu identidad visual, naming, tagline... Innova y activa.

8. Pasa del storytelling al storydoing

Las cosas no se dicen, se hacen. Porque al hacerlas se dicen solas.

9. Predica con el ejemplo

Tu CEO y empleados son tus principales embajadores. No exijas a tus clientes lo que tú no haces.

10. Hazlo porque quieres no porque debes

Más allá del *Greenwashing*. Evidentemente defender cualquier causa justa debe ser desde el propósito. Como un fin genuino y nunca como medio para obtener algo gracias a un dolor ajeno. No seas oportunista.

PLAY THE TOOL

El Mundo sería un lugar mejor si todos pudieran

_____

_____

_____

gracias a ——————————————

_____

_____

¿Cuántos estás activando?

○ **1. Pasa de Just do it a do it good for all**
¿Impactas de forma positiva también en tus "no clientes"?
¿Cómo podrías dar más?

○ **2. Busca beneficios más allá de ingresos**
Además de dinero, ¿qué más estás ganando con tu proyecto?

○ **3. Crea marcas para personas no solo para consumidores**
¿Qué sabes de la persona que hay detrás del cliente?

○ **4. Haz marcas que vivan en este mundo**
¿Resuelves problemas reales del día a día?

○ **5. Sé coherente además de sostenible**
¿Estás activando tu esencia y valores en lo que haces?

○ **6. Defiende causas justas**
¿Tu marca toma partido ante alguna injusticia o conflicto?

○ **7. Trasciende en todos los puntos de contacto**
¿Cómo estás comunicando tu propósito?

○ **8. Pasa del storytelling al storydoing**
¿Qué acciones haces para hacer tangible tu propósito?

○ **9. Predica con el ejemplo**
¿Cómo das ejemplo como CEO?

○ **10. Hazlo porque quieres no porque debes**
¿Lo haces para tener beneficios y buena reputación o por qué de verdad quieres hacerlo?

Purpose score _____ **/10**

PROPÓSITO CHECK

BRAND
VALUES

"Las cosas no se dicen, se hacen, porque al hacerlas no hace falta decirlas"

Woody Allen

SERLO, VIVIRLO Y PARECERLO

¿Qué es?

Los valores de marca son los principios e ideales que guían la forma en la que nos expresamos, actuamos y nos comportamos para que nos perciban como queremos ser percibidos. Hacen real y palpable nuestra propuesta de marca a través de hechos, no solo de palabras.

Expresan lo que creemos como marca y lo que pueden esperar nuestros clientes de nosotros.

Existen dos tipos de valores: funcionales y emocionales.

1. Los valores funcionales: activan nuestro lado más racional. Nos manifiestan cualidades derivadas de la usabilidad del producto o servicio. Son cuantitativos, medibles y objetivos. Como por ejemplo: innovación, fiabilidad, eficacia, rapidez...

2. Los valores emocionales: activan nuestro lado más sentimental. Nos manifiestan sensaciones humanas. Son cualitativos, personales y subjetivos. Como por ejemplo: el respeto, la amabilidad, la comprensión, el cariño...

¿Por qué es importante?

Nuestros valores de marca son aquellos principios que nos mueven. Tangibilizan nuestra promesa. Son la filosofía con la que actuamos tanto interna, como externamente.

Por ejemplo, si predico innovación, un valor, podría ser "Siempre yendo más allá de lo convencional". Esto lo debería transmitir en todo lo que haga como marca. Si quiero trasladar compromiso, mi valor podría ser "Creemos en el poder de la palabra".

Mediante la personificación los consumidores integran como propios los valores de las marcas con las que conectan. Utilizan sus asociaciones positivas como expresión de su propia identidad personal.

Una marca con valores claros, atractivos y representativos hará que los clientes con los que comparte esta visión sean sus amantes y defensores fieles.

MEET THE TOOL ────────────────

VALORES EMOCIONALES Y FUNCIONALES

Una forma de identificar los valores que te representan y que, por lo tanto, se constituyen como los más relevantes para tu consumidor es utilizando esta herramienta de observación, diagnóstico y proyección.

Con estas cuatro preguntas activaremos nuestras dimensiones y podremos declinar nuestros valores.

Buscamos que nuestros valores sean "activos" que expresen algo más que un término estático y descontextualizado.

LAS 4 DIMENSIONES DEL VALUE MAP:

1. Desde un punto de vista social

¿Qué puede esperar la sociedad de ti?

2. Desde el punto de vista de tus públicos

¿Qué pueden esperar tus clientes de ti?

3. Desde un punto de vista aspiracional y motivacional

¿Qué esperas de ti mismo como marca?

4. Desde el punto de vista de tu sector

¿Qué puede esperar tu competencia de ti?

BRAND VALUES

Primero busca la palabra que de respuesta a la pregunta y después activa y tangibiliza el valor.
Te pongo un ejemplo:

¿QUÉ VALOR APORTAS A LA SOCIEDAD?

VALOR:
COMPROMISO

VALOR DECLINADO:
COMPARTIMOS BENEFICIOS

¿QUÉ VALOR APORTAS A TUS CLIENTES?

VALOR:
CONFIANZA

VALOR DECLINADO:
CREEMOS EN EL VALOR DE LA PALABRA

¿QUÉ VALOR TE APORTAS A TI MISMO?

VALOR:
RESISTENCIA

VALOR DECLINADO:
TRANSFORMACIÓN COMO FILOSOFÍA

¿QUÉ VALOR APORTAS A LA COMPETENCIA?

VALOR:
INNOVACIÓN

VALOR DECLINADO:
SIEMPRE BUSCANDO NUEVAS PREGUNTAS

PLAY THE TOOL

¿QUÉ VALOR APORTAS A LA SOCIEDAD?

¿QUÉ VALOR APORTAS A TUS CLIENTES?

¿QUÉ VALOR TE APORTAS A TI MISMO?

¿QUÉ VALOR APORTAS A LA COMPETENCIA?

VALOR:

_____

VALOR ACTIVADO:

_____

VALOR:

_____

VALOR ACTIVADO:

_____

VALOR:

_____

VALOR ACTIVADO:

_____

VALOR:

_____

VALOR ACTIVADO:

_____

BRAND VALUES

AHORA QUE HAS TERMINADO EL DRIVER 3 COMPLETA:
TU ESENCIA Y ADN

CORE VALUE

_____
_____
_____
_____
_____
_____
_____
_____
_____
_____
_____
_____
_____
_____
_____
_____
_____
_____

PROPÓSITO

_____
_____
_____
_____
_____
_____
_____
_____
_____
_____
_____
_____
_____
_____
_____
_____
_____
_____
_____
_____

SIGNIFICAR ES AMAR · SIMBOLIZAR UNA PASIÓN · UN PROPÓSITO REAL · ENAMORAR Y FIDELIZAR

EN UN VISTAZO

POSICIONAMIENTO

VALORES

VALOR 1

VALOR 2

VALOR 3

VALOR 4

SIGNIFICAR ES AMAR · SIMBOLIZAR UNA PASIÓN · UN PROPÓSITO REAL · ENAMORAR Y FIDELIZAR

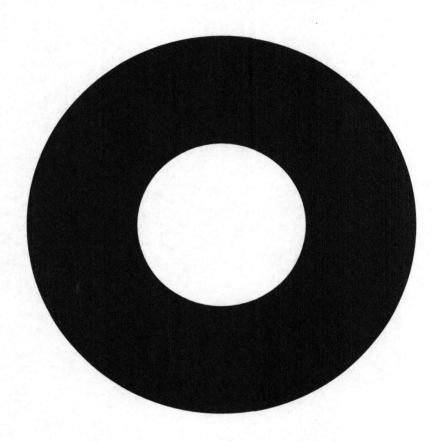

THE BRAND IDENTITY

IDENTIDAD Y ACTIVOS DE MARCA

DRIVER 4 · ACTIVOS DE MARCA
THE BRAND IDENTITY

"Listen to what people don't say"

Steve DeMasco

"Oíd lo que los demás no dicen"

¿PARA QUÉ SIRVE UNA MARCA?
PUES PARA DIFERENCIAR TU VACA DE LA MÍA

La palabra *brand* -marca en inglés- viene de *burn*, literalmente *"mark with a hot iron"*. Marcar en español, también. Es la palabra que utilizamos para señalar a nuestro ganado. Pero ¿por qué lo hacemos?

Estas marcas existen básicamente para saber qué vaca es la mía y qué vaca es la tuya. Para que se puedan distinguir de forma fácil en una vaquería homogénea -donde todas las vacas son "iguales"-. Las cosas son más simples de lo que pueden parecer.

Muchos años después, seguimos usando a las "marcas" para el mismo fin: **identificarnos para poder diferenciarnos.**

Si lo piensas, para eso sirven básicamente los logos, que no dejan de ser la evolución de las marcas a fuego del ganado, solo que estampados en productos o servicios.

¡Pero atención! Una marca no es un logo.

El logo es un buen representante de la identidad visual pero no el único. Es fácil distinguir una marca de otra cuando vemos su logo y nos es conocido. Pero aquí viene lo interesante ¿Si tapamos el logo de tu marca tus audiencias podrían reconocerte? ¿Sabrían que sigues siendo tú?

Si tu respuesta es no, estás perdiendo el 90% de tus oportunidades y fortalezas como marca ya que, además de la identidad visual, existen 4 identidades más que activar y potenciar.

Te pongo un ejemplo. Piensa en una persona -en alguien que conozcas bien- seguramente, le podrías reconocer por su voz, por su estilo de vestir e incluso por sus ideales o costumbres. Podrías incluso saber si ha estado en tu casa por como ha dejado de desordenado u ordenado el entorno donde ha interactuado.

Con las marcas ocurre lo mismo. Tienen voz, forma y "actos". Debemos iconizar, destacar y comunicar al máximo sus fortalezas y particularidades que las hacen únicas para capitalizarlas. Todos los activos tangibles e intangibles de los que dispones son una oportunidad de impactar, conectar y vender que no debes dejar escapar.

Solo se existe cuándo te piensan.

AQUÍ TE PRESENTO LAS 5 IDENTIDADES DE LAS QUE ESTÁN COMPUESTAS TODAS LAS MARCAS Y QUE DEBEMOS CAPITALIZAR AL MÁXIMO:

Identidad visual: Activación a través de nuestra imagen.

Identidad verbal: Activación a través de nuestro discurso y verbo.

Identidad simbólica: Activación a través de nuestras asociaciones e ideales.

Identidad actitudinal: Activación a través de nuestra personalidad y actos.

Identidad sensorial: Activación a través de nuestros sentidos.

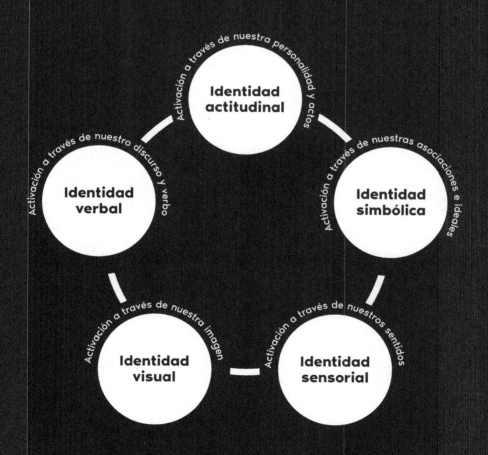

"Una marca es mucho más que un logo"

En un libro de branding no podía faltar esta famosísima y célebre frase, tampoco la Comic Sans :P

El logo importa -pero no lo es todo-. En mi agencia decimos que vendemos marcas y regalamos logos.

Trabajamos todos los proyectos bajo la idea de la trinidad. Una marca está formada por tres dimensiones que se complementan y equilibran, sin las cuales la marca no sería competitiva:

BRAND
CREATIVE

BRAND
ESSENCE

BRAND
COMMUNICATION

Nuestra activación e identidad es transversal a las tres dimensiones. Debe construir y potenciar cada parte. Sin una de estas nuestra marca estará coja.

UNA TRINIDAD EQUILIBRADA

OÍD LO QUE LOS DEMÁS NO DICEN. TODO, TODO Y TODO COMUNICA

Aquí viene otra cosa muy importante -que a veces no caemos en ella- los puntos de contacto o los espacios a activar.

La marca y sus 5 identidades -verbal, visual, actitudinal, sensorial y simbólica- deben estar presentes en todos los elementos y acciones con lo que tengan contacto tus audiencias. Tangibles o intangibles.

Desde la web, el packaging, el uniforme de trabajo hasta cómo habla nuestro asistente virtual, todo cuenta.

Activar nuestras 5 identidades en todos los puntos de contacto será la diferencia entre una buena marca y una marca inolvidablemente buena.

DRIVER 4 · 5 HERRAMIENTAS PARA DISEÑAR LAS 5 IDENTIDADES DE MARCA: VISUAL, VERBAL, ACTITUDINAL, SIMBÓLICA Y SENSORIAL

TOOL 1 · THE BRAND SYMBOL
¿QUÉ REPRESENTAS? · IDENTIDAD SIMBÓLICA

TOOL 2 · BRAND CHARISMA ARCHETYPES
¿CÓMO ACTÚAS? · IDENTIDAD ACTITUDINAL

TOOL 3 · TONE OF VOICE PATH
¿CÓMO COMUNICAS? · IDENTIDAD VERBAL

TOOL 4 · FULL BRAND BOARD
¿CÓMO EVOCAS? · IDENTIDAD VISUAL

TOOL 5 · THE SENSE SQUARE
¿QUÉ SIENTES? · IDENTIDAD SENSORIAL

BENEFICIOS DE ACTIVAR EL DRIVER:

- Potenciar todos nuestros activos: tangibles e intangibles
- Crear una experiencia completa
- Diferenciarnos de la competencia
- Innovar en significados y experiencias
- Construir una marca más clara y homogénea
- Reducir el gap entre imagen e identidad
- Impactar y sorprender con elementos únicos e inimitables

THE
BRAND
SYMBOL

LAS ▬▬▬ IDEAS NO SON ▬▬▬ DE ▬▬▬ NADIE. ▬▬▬ LAS COSAS NO ▬▬▬ EXISTEN.

ELEMENTOS VEHICULARES. CAPITALIZANDO NUESTRO EQUITY

ACTIVA TU IDENTIDAD SIMBÓLICA. CAPITALIZA Y FOMENTA TUS ASOCIACIONES POSITIVAS

Nuestro consumo es simbólico. Compras significados e ideales pero consumes productos y materia. Compras *eidos*, consumes *ousía*.

¿Qué es?

Bienvenido a la era del *Brand Symbolism*. Las marcas pueden ser capaces de representar mucho más que lo que percibimos. Se componen de significados inmutables, que forman parte de un inconsciente colectivo universal. (Belleza, amor, felicidad, poder...)

Las marcas como símbolo han ayudado a forjar la personalidad de sus consumidores aportándoles valores y formas de autoexpresión. Portar una u otra marca es una forma de comunicar mediante símbolos quién se es o cómo se quiere ser visto.

Las marcas más poderosas son las que son asociadas a ideales atemporales y poseen activos inmateriales además de tangibles.

También, una marca, puede ser la representación y espejo de la sociedad, de las generaciones en el momento de su creación y de los valores admirados culturalmente.

Un ejemplo célebre es Coca-Cola como icono de nuestra sociedad y sus vanguardias. Destapa la felicidad, ¿no?.

¿Por qué es importante?

Uniéndose y mimetizándose con los valores de una marca es más fácil para algunas personas sentirse acogido o construir una personalidad de cara a los otros.

Mediante los símbolos, ideales y rituales que existen detrás de las marcas los consumidores se acercan a una relación casi mitológica con ellas. Pasando de ser clientes a devotos.

Como gestores de marca podemos potenciar, tangibilizar y medir esta identidad.

Haz que se entreguen al mito de tu marca. Permíteles hacer realidad todos sus sueños y deseos. Que se olviden que la magia tiene precio.

MEET THE TOOL ─────────────

Podríamos llamar a esta dimensión el patrimonio inmaterial de las marcas. Debemos capitalizar todos nuestros recursos y dotar a nuestros clientes de significados y experiencias valiosas. Nuestra marca debe tener sus símbolos, ideales, rituales y asociaciones bien definidos. Para ilustrar esta herramienta me gustaría que pienses en ROSALÍA, la cantante española. Mi favorita.

LAS 4 DIMENSIONES SIMBÓLICAS DE LAS MARCAS:

1. IDEALES DE MARCA - LO QUE REPRESENTAS
Los principios atemporales o valores inmutables que aspira alcanzar tu marca y que trasladas a tus audiencias.

Ej: MOTOMAMI es su actitud hacia el Mundo. Libertad y poder son sus ideales atemporales.

2. ASOCIACIONES DE MARCA - LO QUE TRANSCIENDES
Elementos no vinculados directamente con tu actividad o producto que capitalizas como propios y buscas que se te asocie a aspectos positivos de ellos.

Ej: en el caso de ROSALÍA vemos el mundo del motor de forma constante. Vinculándose a su persona la fuerza y potencia. También a la marca España con color rojo y pasión.

3. SÍMBOLOS - LO QUE CONSTRUYES
Representaciones perceptible y tangible de ideas mediante elementos identificativos propios. Materializas tus ideales, los bajas a la tierra.

Ej: mariposa, casco de moto, pelo negro, uñas largas como símbolo de poderío.

4. RITOS Y COSTUMBRES - LO QUE VIVES
Acciones y experiencias, guionizadas, propias y únicas que se repiten con un fin.

Ej: su trá trá con las manos o el sonido de motor en sus canciones.

THE BRAND SYMBOL

IDEALES DE MARCA

Tus principios y valores a seguir. Lo que representas.

MOTOMAMI = LIBERTAD + PODERÍO

ASOCIACIONES DE MARCA

Elementos ajenos a tu sector que capitalizas como propios. Lo que trasciendes.

MUNDO DEL MOTOR

SÍMBOLOS

Significados, modelos universales. Lo que construyes.

PELO, UÑAS, MARIPOSA...

RITOS Y COSTUMBRES

Experiencias y acciones propias. Lo que vives.

TRÁ, TRÁ + MOTOR

Construye una identidad simbólica fácil de entender, de ilustrar y de interpretar.

Apropiarse de una idea, concepto o recursos agradable para elevar e impregnar nuestra marca de esas asociaciones positivas. Cuánto más universal y fácil de entender mejor.

PLAY THE TOOL

IDEALES DE MARCA

Tus principios y valores a seguir.
Lo que representas.

_____
_____
_____

SÍMBOLOS

Significados, modelos universales.
Lo que construyes.

_____
_____
_____

ASOCIACIONES DE MARCA

Elementos ajenos a tu sector que capitalizas
como propios. Lo que transciendes.

_____

_____

_____

RITOS Y COSTUMBRES

Experiencias y acciones propias.
Lo que vives.

_____

_____

_____

THE BRAND SYMBOL

BRAND
CHARISMA
ARCHETYPES

¿ERES LO QUE COMPRAS?

¿Qué es?

Somos consumidores posmodernos y una característica de la posmodernidad es la fragmentación. Creamos nuestra identidad mediante diferentes objetos o piezas de consumo.

Piensa en todas las marcas que te rodean ahora mismo y en las que llevas puestas. Imagina que cada una de ellas es una pieza de un puzzle. Cuando unes todas las piezas, ¿qué imagen te muestra el puzzle formado? Inconscientemente eso es lo que eres, o quieres ser.

Las marcas son percibidas como contenedores de significados, a través de los cuales, alcanzamos objetivos emocionales personales. Refutan y nos ayudan a expresar nuestro papel como individuos. También, el que queremos representar en la sociedad afirmando y reforzando nuestra identidad -self- e ilustrando nuestra imagen.

Compras lo que eres.

Por eso -a mismo precio y funcionalidades- la elección estará vinculada directamente a tu propia personalidad, siendo las marcas una proyección de la misma.

Buscaremos aquello que nos represente y potencie como individuos. Marcas "de nuestra tribu" "como nosotros" o "de nosotros".

¿Por qué es importante?
Deja claro a tus clientes a qué tribu les harás pertenecer.

Podemos definir la personalidad como diferencia individual que constituye a cada persona y la distingue de otra. También como conjunto de características o cualidades originales que destacan en algunas personas.

Como vemos, la identidad actitudinal

¿O COMPRAS LO QUE ERES?

es uno de los activos más importantes de nuestra marca. Debe ser gestionada con coherencia y atención.

Cuanto más aumenta nuestro nivel de vida, más propensos somos a buscar un estatus mediante el consumo de símbolos. Este fenómeno fue primeramente observado por Velben (1929) al darse cuenta de la relación existente de una nueva clase social americana y de un nuevo consumo al que llamó **consumo conspicuo**, donde los individuos buscaban una adquisición de productos que les diferenciara socialmente.

Por lo tanto, tener una personalidad de marca clara será fundamental para atraer a un público de similares características. Es necesario que el consumidor asocie su personalidad con la de la marca para crear una vinculación y admiración real. Si queremos que nos consuman personas cuidadosas debemos ser una marca cuidadosa, si buscamos que nos consuman rebeldes debemos ser una marca rebelde. Serlo, y parecerlo.

MERCEDES: DEL COCHE DE TU PADRE AL COCHE DE MODA

Un ejemplo de personalidad de marca unido a competitividad y posicionamiento de negocio fue Mercedes. Mediante la personificación de un embajador más joven y rebelde como el chef Dabiz Muñoz logró pasar de interesar a un segmento de edad senior a jóvenes consumidores. Un cambio claro de posicionamiento vinculado la identidad actitudinal sin perder su estatus y posicionamiento de marca.

Todas las marcas independientemente del sector pueden y deben tener una personalidad definida.

No hay excusas, si no que se lo digan a la fabada de Litoral y a su abuela trapera.

MEET THE TOOL

El carisma se define como cualidad o don natural que tiene una persona para atraer a los demás por su presencia, su palabra o su personalidad. Y eso es justamente lo que buscamos hacer mediante la gestión de la personalidad de nuestra marca.

Definimos 12 arquetipos de personalidad de marca en base a dos variables:

1. EL CAMBIO O LA ESTABILIDAD
2. LA COLECTIVIDAD O EL INDIVIDUALISMO

Aquí mis 12 arquetipos y carismas de marca.
Una reinvención y adaptación de los de Jenifer Aaker.
¿Cuáles te representan?

1. THE RADICAL:
Te da rebeldía. Para romper con lo establecido y correcto, sin tabúes.
Marcas como Diverxo.

2. THE HERO:
Te da valor, fuerza y poder. Para transformarte.
Marcas como Nike.

3. THE LIBERATOR:
Te da liberación. Para ser quien tú quieras.
Marcas como Desigual.

4. THE PLAYFULL:
Te da diversión. Para que pases un buen rato con picaresca y alegría.
Marcas como Netflix.

5. THE HEDONIST:
Te da placer. Para que disfrutes y te deleites con la vida.
Marcas como Rituals.

6. THE SAFER:
Te da seguridad. Para que te sientas bien y a salvo, te cuida.
Marcas como Volvo.

BRAND CHARISMA ARCHETYPES

CAMBIO

INDIVIDUALISMO

COLECTIVIDAD

ESTABILIDAD

 7. THE RULER:
Te da estatus, poder y distinción. Para mantener tu superioridad.
Marcas como JP Morgan.

 8. THE MASTER:
Te da maestría. Para exponer tu experiencia y saber hacer.
Marcas como Lindt.

 9. THE WISE:
Te da conocimiento. Para obtener soluciones y respuestas.
Marcas como Google.

 10. THE HUMAN:
Te da pertenencia y unión. Para que conectes con los otros.
Marcas como Ikea.

 11. THE COMMITTED:
Te da compromiso. Para afrontar causas justas.
Marcas como Toms.

 12. THE VISIONARY:
Te da visión. Para transformar lo corriente en extraordinario.
Marcas como Tesla.

PLAY THE TOOL

INDIVIDUALISMO

The Radical

Te da rebeldía. Para romper con lo esestablecido y correcto, sin tabúes.

The Hero

Te da valor, fuerza y poder. Para transformarte.

The Liberator

Te da liberación. Para ser quien tú quieras.

The Smiling

Te da diversión. Para que pases un buen rato con picaresca y alegría.

The Hedonist

Te da placer. Para que disfrutes y te deleites con la vida.

The Safer

Te da seguridad. Para que te sientas bien y a salvo, te cuida.

CAMBIO

The Visionary

Te da visión. Para transformar lo corriente en extraordinario.

The Commited

Te da compromiso. Para afrontar causas justas.

The Human

Te da pertenencia y unión. Para que conectes con los otros.

The Wise

Te da conocimiento. Para obtener soluciones y respuestas.

The Master

Te da maestría. Para exponer tu experiencia y saber hacer.

The Ruler

Te da estatus, poder y distinción. Para mantener tu superioridad.

ESTABILIDAD

COLECTIVIDAD

BRAND CHARISMA ARCHETYPES

	The Radical ⚡	The Hero ⊛	The Liberator 🦋	The Smiling :)	The Hedonist ♥	The Safer 🛡
LEMA O MOTTO	Te da rebeldía. Para romper con lo establecido y correcto, sin tabúes.	Te da valor, fuerza y poder. Para transformarte.	Te da liberación. Para ser quien tú quieras.	Te da diversión. Para que pases un buen rato, picaresca, alegría.	Te da placer. Para que disfrutes y te deleites con la vida.	Te da seguridad. Para que te sientas bien y a salvo, te cuida.
MIEDO	**SER ORDINARIO**	**SER DÉBIL**	**SER SOMETIDO**	**SER ABURRIDO**	**SER PRIVADO**	**SER FALSO**
ATRIBUTOS	Disturbar, impactar y llamar la atención.	Competencia, ímpetu y coraje.	Originalidad, autoexpresión y libertad.	Alegría de vivir, buen humor y jugar.	Pasión, disfrute del momento y deleite.	Seguridad, compromiso, lealtad.
MARCAS QUE...	Rompen con los convencionalismos de la industria. Tienen una filosofía y visión salvaje y sin tabúes. Habla sin miedo. Vive sin límites.	Animan a superar un reto y buscar la excelencia personal. Empoderan y ayudan a alcanzar objetivos. Acompañan en la superación.	Potencian la autenticidad y autoexpresión. Ayudar al consumidor a expresar su identidad e individualismo.	Te hacen pasar un buen rato animando y divertido. Hablan desde el LOL, el buen humor y la alegría de vivir.	Marcas sibaritas que buscan el placer y el disfrute a través de la experiencia. Hacen que el consumidor se entregue a la experiencia sin arrepentimientos.	Cuidan a su consumidor, les aportan seguridad y continuidad sobre sus costumbres. Les dan fiabilidad sobre sus decisiones. Marcas siempre leales, marcas que cumplen sus promesas.
	DIVERXO VICIO	NIKE DOVE	DOVE DESIGUAL	NETFLIX VUELING	RITUALS CHOCOLATE VALOR	VOLVO BIMBO

The Ruler ♛	The Master ♞	The Wise ⚛	The Human 👣	The Commited ❋	The Visionary 🚀
Te da estatus, poder y distinción. Para mantener tu superioridad.	Te da maestría. Para exponer tu experiencia y saber hacer.	Te da conocimiento. Para obtener soluciones y respuestas.	Te da pertenencia y unión. Para que conectes con los otros.	Te da compromiso. Para afrontar causas justas.	Te da visión. Para transformar lo corriente en extraordinario.
SER DESBANCADO	**SER OLVIDADO**	**SER ERRÓNEO**	**SER AISLADO**	**SER INÚTIL**	**SER FRACASADO**
Diferenciación, exclusividad y poder.	Legado, experiencia, *know how* y método.	Conocimiento, descubrimiento e innovación.	Conexión, pertenencia democratización, empatía y unión.	Compromiso, propósito, principios.	Transformación, excentricidad, creatividad.
Buscan que sus consumidores se diferencien de los otros mediante el éxito y liderazgo.\n\nOfrecen productos o servicios utilizados para demostrar su poder.	Marcas que cuentan con trayectorias históricas que les han posicionado como referentes y maestros.\n\nCuentan con un sólido saber hacer y experiencia propia.	Se cetran en la búsqueda de información y conocimiento.\n\nLa autoreflexión y la comprensión de los procesos del pensamiento.	Buscan que sus productos sean accesibles para la mayor parte de consumidores.\n\nAbre las puertas a todo tipo de perfiles, democratiza.	Buscan crear una comunidad por la defensa de ciertos principios y valores que comparten.\n\nSe diferencian del resto por estar "haciendo las cosas bien".\n\nLuchan mendiante su consumo contra injusticias.	Marcas que diseñan lo aún desconocido.\n\nCreativas, transforman lo común en extraordinario.\n\nReplantean su entorno y lo transforman.\n\nRompen moldes.\n\nInnovación como cultura.
J.P MORGAN HERMES	LINDT CHOCOLATES OSBORNE	GOOGLE MICROSOFT	IKEA MCDONALDS	PATAGONIA TOMS	SPACE X APPLE

TONE OF
VOICE
PATH

"La gente olvidará lo que dijiste, olvidará lo que hiciste, pero nunca olvidarán lo que les hiciste sentir"

Maya Angelou

NO SOLO ES LO QUE DICES, SI NO CÓMO LO DICES
LA FORMA QUE TIENE TU MARCA DE COMUNICARSE Y CREAR RELACIONES.

¿Qué es?

La identidad verbal es cómo expresamos lo que somos mediante el lenguaje y sus mensajes. Esta identidad dota de elementos reconocibles, únicos y replicables a nuestra marca. Al igual que la identidad visual hace identificable una marca, la identidad verbal debe tiene la misma función. Por ejemplo, si tapásemos el logo de una creatividad, nuestras audiencias mediante palabras clave, estructuras del lenguaje o personalidad sabrán que somos nosotros.

¿Por qué es importante?

Gracias a la identidad verbal, hacemos palpable nuestra personalidad, la hacemos creíble. Nos ayuda a establecer relaciones más humanas y da un carácter único a nuestra historia.

Nos posiciona y diferencia de la competencia a la vez que aporta coherencia a nuestro posicionamiento. Nuestra identidad verbal debe adaptarse a nuestras audiencias y ser aplicada en todos los puntos de contacto.

Una identidad verbal competitiva debe ser consistente y única. Debe nacer de lo que somos y de cómo somos. Tiene que motivar a tus clientes a conectar con tu marca, sintiéndose representados.

Escribe como hablas.

MEET THE TOOL

6 ELEMENTOS CLAVE PARA CONSTRUIR LA IDENTIDAD VERBAL DE TU MARCA

1. TONO DE VOZ:

El tono nace de la personalidad. Es el carácter de tu marca. Como se relaciona con el Mundo y como actúa en él. De somos xxx a hablamos xxx **Nos define.**

2. VOICE LAND:

El territorio que engloba y define cómo vamos a plasmar nuestra personalidad en todo lo que decimos y en cómo lo decimos. Guía nuestra forma de expresarnos y sirve de medida y filtro para saber si estamos *on brand.* De cómo somos a cómo hablamos. De actuar a comunicar. **Nos guía.**

3. VOICE PATH:

Las guías de estilo. Las normas y formas que tenemos que respetar. Son nuestro marco de actuación verbal y las indicaciones a seguir. **Nos aportan homogeneidad y coherencia.**

4. RECURSOS DIFERENCIALES:

Estructuras, composiciones, mensajes de alto impacto que repetimos. Si no está nuestro logo, esta estructura debería de ser igualmente reconocible por nuestros consumidores. **Nos representan y diferencian.**

5. PALABRAS CLAVE/PROHIBIDA:

Las palabras clave son aquellas que queremos destacar, posicionar en la mente de nuestros consumidores. Las potenciamos y remarcamos siempre que sea posible. Las palabras prohibidas son aquellas evitamos utilizar ya que están siendo capitalizadas por la competencia. **Nos posicionan.**

6. APLICACIONES Y OPORTUNIDADES:

No nos podemos olvidar de pasar de la teoría a la práctica. Hay que activar todos aquellos espacios donde podemos aplicar y potenciar nuestra identidad verbal. **Nos activan.**

VOICE LAND

>>Imaginemos que somos un restaurante mexicano.

TONO DE VOZ
¿Cómo nos comunicamos?

SOMOS SIMPÁTICOS – TONO SIMPÁTICO

NOS DEFINE

VOICE LAND - TERRITORIO VERBAL
¿Qué deben transmitir siempre tus mensajes?

ALWAYS GOOD MOOD

NOS GUÍA

VOICE PATH - GUÍAS DE ESTILO
¿Qué guías y parámetros deben cumplir?

1. SIEMPRE HABLAMOS CON BUEN HUMOR Y ENERGÍA PERO SIN SER GRITONES O FALTONES

2. EVITAMOS EL USO DE FRASES NEGATIVAS QUE EMPIECEN POR PROHIBICIONES

NOS DA COHERENCIA

RECURSOS DIFERENCIALES	**PALABRA CLAVE / PROHIBIDA**	**APLICACIONES**
DOBLE O EN NUESTROS PRODUCTOS ESTRELLA: *MOOJITO MOOD* *GOOD BURRITOO*	*PALABRA CLAVE:* *GOOD* *PALABRA PROHIBIDA:* *TASTY*	*MANTEL, SERVILLETA, GORRA DEL REPARTIDOR, PEGATINAS PARA EL ORDENADOR...*
NOS DIFERENCIA	**NOS POSICIONA**	**NOS ACTIVA**

PLAY THE TOOL

TONO DE VOZ
¿Cómo nos comunicamos?

NOS DEFINE

VOICE LAND - TERRITORIO VERBAL
¿Qué deben transmitir siempre tus mensajes?

NOS GUÍA

VOICE PATH - GUÍA DE ESTILO
¿Qué guías y parámetros deben cumplir?

NOS DA COHERENCIA

RECURSOS DIFERENCIALES

NOS DIFERENCIA

PALABRA CLAVE / PROHIBIDA

NOS POSICIONA

APLICACIONES

NOS ACTIVA

TONE OF VOICE PATH

NAMING

CUENTA AL MUNDO QUE HAS LLEGADO

DIME CÓMO TE LLAMAS Y TE DIRÉ QUIÉN ERES
DIME QUIÉN ERES Y ENCONTRARÉ TU EIDOS

Una de las escenas más eclécticas de mi infancia es cuando Alicia se encuentra con la oruga morada en el País de las Maravillas y esta le pregunta: *Who are you?* ¿Quién eres tú?

¿Qué es?

Y aquí estamos muchos años después reflexionando sobre esa escena maestra de Disney y todo el valor que ha aportado al branding. Entonces, *Who are you?*

Cuando alguien te pregunta quién eres tu respuesta por lo general es decir tu nombre. Totalmente normal, ya que el nombre es tu primera presentación al mundo y una de las más importantes. A lo largo de tu vida podrás cambiar de estilo o incluso de forma pero es mucho más difícil cambiar de nombre. Lo mismo ocurre con las marcas, puedes cambiar de logo pero será mucho más complejo cambiar de nombre

¿Por qué es importante?

Nombrar marcas es uno de mis artes favoritos, pero sin duda el más difícil. Debes partir siempre de un nombre que te represente, del que sentirte orgulloso.

Nuestro nombre es un valor intangible que supera las fluctuaciones del mercado, las evoluciones y modificaciones del entorno, de la tecnología cambiante y de las modas.

Un nombre competitivo debe ser:

1. Reconocible: Fortalece e impulsa la notoriedad de la marca.

2. Evocador: Transmite el concepto de marca a través de asociaciones positivas.

3. Memorable: Provoca la identificación y aumenta la diferenciación frente a la competencia.

4. Único: Es diferente a todo lo que existe en tu mercado.

5. Global: Un nombre capaz de afrontar la internacionalización de la marca, pero que a la vez genere *engagement* local.

Truco de brander: evita letras características de ciertos territorios ya que no aparecerán en los teclados de tus clientes, por ejemplo Ñ, Ç ...

MEET THE TOOL

Todos los nombres se pueden dividir en las siguientes 6 tipologías. Explora opciones hasta encontrar el nombre más competitivo para tu proyecto.
Una vez que tengas seleccionada tu Short List recuerda hacer un análisis de competencia y un análisis legal para ver si puedes utilizar ese nombre.

FUNDADORES
Nombres que hacen referencia a los creadores de la marca o al lugar de origen.

Juancho's BBQ, Ben & Jerry's, Ralph Lauren o Banco Santander

DESCRIPTIVOS
Nombres que describen algún elemento de la actividad o producto.

Basque Culinary Center, Car2go o Compramostucoche.com

EVOCADORES
Nombres que se inspiran en algo relacionado con la actividad sin ser puramente descriptivos.

Google, Tesla, Grata Maison, Diverxo o Iberia

NAMING

ABSTRACTOS
Nombres que propone una nueva realidad distinta a la natural u original de la palabra utilizada.
Apple, Mango, Windows o Amazon. Apple la marca tecnológica no vende manzanas. Aunque según Jobs "I like apples and it comes ahead of Atari in the phone book"

ACRÓNIMOS
Nombres formados por la unión de elementos de dos o más palabras, siglas o letras.
BBVA (Banco Bilbao Bizcaya Argentaria) , MoMA (Museum of Modern Art) o KFC (Kentucky Fried Chicken)

FANTASÍA
Nombres inventados, que no significan nada. Creados para diferenciarse de todo lo que existe y evocar elementos valiosos mediante sus fonemas.
Häagen-Dazs (marca de NY que buscaba parecer nórdica)

NO PODEMOS OLVIDAR OTROS GRANDES ACTIVOS VERBALES

Diferencia como un buen brander un tagline de un slogan.

Las palabras condenan o liberan. Crean el Mundo. Lo que no puedes expresar no existe. Cuenta al Mundo que has llegado.

Te cuento una curiosidad: un tesauro es una lista de palabras o términos empleados para representar conceptos. Proviene del latín *thesaurus*, y este a su vez del griego clásico thēsaurós. Es utilizado en literatura como thesaurus, thesauri o tesoro para referirse a los diccionarios.

Usa bien el poder de las palabras, son el verdadero tesoro de las marcas.

Usamos un tagline o un slogan para de forma breve, memorable y potente comunicar todo nuestro valor. Parecen lo mismo, pero no se usan igual.

TAGLINE

Acompaña a nuestra marca de forma estratégica, sintetiza nuestra esencia y será nuestro mantra para lograr nuestros objetivos. Suele acompañar al logotipo.

BMW - BEYOND RATIONAL.
NIKE - JUST DO IT.

SLOGAN
O CLAIM

Lo utilizamos de forma táctica en
publicidad para ilustrar una campaña en
particular de la marca.

**BMW - ¿TE GUSTA CONDUCIR?
NIKE - PLAY NEW**

213

FULL
BRAND
BOARD

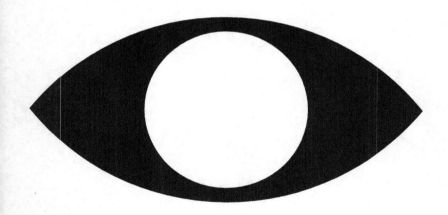

LA DICTADURA DE LA ESTÉTICA O LO REAL

NO HAY UNA SEGUNDA OPORTUNIDAD PARA UNA PRIMERA IMPRESIÓN

Debemos impactar con consistencia y significado, haciendo que nuestra propuesta trascienda y sea memorable. ¿Una imagen vale más que mil palabras?

¿Qué es?

Que entre por los ojos, que erice la piel. Nuestra identidad visual debe ser relevante pero a la vez inesperada. Debe generar emoción, expectación y admiración en el consumidor. Pero también debe ser consistente y armónica ya que el carácter de la marca debe ser representado de forma homogénea en todos sus puntos de contacto.

Ten en cuenta que la construcción de elementos gráficos y visuales ha de estar al servicio de la marca -sus valores y su posicionamiento- no solo representar una tendencia.

La identidad visual es un *asset*. Un punto de activación de nuestra marca, no al revés. Es un elemento más de comunicación, no el único.

¿Por qué es importante?

Nuestros activos visuales nos identifican y diferencian. Partiendo de nuestro *asset* más célebre, el logo, hasta nuestros emojis, colores o patrones... todo es una oportunidad de comunicar lo que somos a través de lo que parecemos.

No es nada personal. Una identidad visual competitiva transciende modas y gustos personales. Enfoca la creación y tus decisiones exclusivamente a la competitividad de la marca, las demandas de tu entorno y tu mercado. Estrategas si, opinadores no, gracias.

Una imagen vale más que mil palabras. Más bien, evoca más que mil palabras. Te pongo un ejemplo. Piensa en qué tipo de comida vendería este restaurante. Aquí solo hemos jugado con el poder de la tipografía.

CAROLINA'S TASTE

CAROLINA'S TASTE

Carolina´s Taste

Una identidad visual debe acompañar y potenciar nuestra esencia de marca. Fomentar su identidad -lo que eres- a través de su imagen -lo que pareces-.

La identidad de marca puede estar presente en infinidad de soportes.

Todo comunica. Si vamos a tener -por ejemplo- papelería corporativa, el papel seleccionado también comunica. Si somos una marca con valores de ecología y sostenibilidad, no podemos escoger un papel brillante y blanco porque no sería coherente con nuestros valores.

Como dice la famosa frase:

"ADEMÁS DE SERLO HAY QUE PARECERLO"

¿CUÁNTO ME COBRAS POR UN LOGO?

Seguro que si eres un diseñador te han hecho esta pregunta alguna vez. Como decimos en mi agencia, hacemos marcas y regalamos logos. Pero ya que estamos te dejo algunas claves que debe tener un buen logotipo.

LOS 5 MUST DE TODO LOGO

1 Que sea sencillo y que funcione en pequeño y gran formato.

2 Que esté alineado con la esencia de marca.
Ej. Si es una marca delicada o enfocada a cuidados, evitar los ángulos pronunciados y picos. Apuesta por curvas o formas suaves y sutiles.

3 Que funcione a una tinta o dos tintas. Me lo agradecerás a la hora de imprimir.

4 El logo es un distintivo y debe cumplir su función principal: diferenciarte e identificarte.

5 Que represente a la marca no solo a la persona detrás de ella.

MEET THE TOOL & PLAY

¿CÓMO SERÍA SU CASA?

Una forma que uso para definir el universo visual de una marca antes de empezar un proyecto de identidad visual es imaginarme que la marca es una persona y me invita a su casa. Me imagino entrando en su mundo.

Visualizo el estilo de la decoración, de las habitaciones, de los muebles, de las texturas y los colores que veo allí.

El entorno donde está la casa y que sensaciones o impactos visuales recibo. Esto me ayuda a hacerme una primera idea de como desarrollar el proyecto.

Ahora, tú. La puerta está abierta ¿Entras?

FULL BRAND BOARD

SU LOGOTIPO

SU SÍMBOLO	**SU COLOR**
SU TIPOGRAFÍA	**SU LAYOUT**
SUS ILUSTRACIONES	**SU MOTION**
SU FOTOGRAFÍA	**SUS ICONOS**
SUS EMOJIS	**SUS STICKERS**

THE
SENSE
SQUARE

¿A QUÉ SABE LA SUERTE?

SIENTE TU MARCA, ESCUCHA SU PODER

Si te digo que pienses en Nokia seguramente antes de
visualizar el teléfono has escuchado su sonido -na na na na, na
na na na na, na na na na náaa- esto, se llama Sonic Branding y
todas las marcas pueden desarrollarlo.

¿Qué es?

La identidad sensorial de tu marca está compuesta por todos
los activos que percibimos por los sentidos: oído, tacto, gusto,
olfato y evidentemente vista.

Alcanza todo el pontencial de tu identidad sensorial:

SONIC BRANDING -   Activa tu marca a través del sonido

AROMA BRANDING - Activa tu marca a través del olor

TASTE BRANDING -   Activa tu marca a través de los sabores

TOUCH BRANDING -   Activa tu marca a través del tacto

VISUAL BRANDING - Activa tu marca a través de la vista

¿Por qué es importante?

La vista la tenemos muy entrenada, por eso, es interesante
activar el resto de sentidos.

Seduce e impacta al cerebro más primitivo de tus clientes a
través del olor y el tacto. Haz que te reconozcan a través del
gingle de tu marca. Crea una sinfonía única y representativa.
La música comunica y emociona, utiliza todo su poder para
exponer lo que eres.

MEET THE TOOL
& PLAY

**Sorprende a tus clientes con una marca
que se siente con los 5 sentidos**

Taste Branding

¿A qué sabría tu marca?
¿Qué sabores la representan?

Sonic Branding

¿Qué música tendría tu marca?
¿Qué sonidos la representan?

THE SENSE SQUARE

Visual Branding

El peso visual de tu marca lo determina su identidad
visual como hemos visto en la tool anterior.

Aroma Branding

¿Qué olor tendría tu marca?
¿Qué aromas la representan?

Touch Branding

¿Qué tacto tendría tu marca?
¿Qué texturas la representan?

IDENTIDAD

SOY...

Y LO PAREZCO
GRACIAS A...

IMAGEN

THE
BRAND
EXPERIENCE

ACTIVACIÓN Y EXPERIENCIA DE MARCA

"The whole World is a single flower"

Seung Sahn

El Mundo entero es una flor.

SÉ EL GRAN ESCENARIO DE TUS CLIENTES

Luces, música y acción. Las marcas nos proporcionan espacios de expresión.

Son el teatro, escenario y atrezo ideal para que podamos interpretar el papel que ansiamos como individuos. Nos ponen buena música para que nosotros bailemos.

Ponle las cosas fáciles a tus clientes. Haz que puedan disfrutar gracias a ti. Que tu marca sea una atracción en sí misma, valiosa para ellos pero también para todo su ecosistema.

Haz que tu marca viva, materialízala y dale forma para el Mundo. Crea una experiencia completa a través de ella. Crea elementos que potencien su esencia y hagan que tus clientes entablen relaciones a largo plazo con ella. Haz que sean tus altavoces.

Pasa de ideas a acciones tangibles. Haz que tu marca se diferencie de tu competencia para aumentar su valor y visibilidad.

Cuéntale y enséñale al Mundo que has llegado. Recuerda: no hay una segunda oportunidad para una primera impresión.

Sé exigente, sé auténtico, sé valiente. Ya hemos llegado.

Tú pones la música, nosotros bailamos.

DRIVER 5 · 5 HERRAMIENTAS PARA ACTIVAR TU ESTRATEGIA DE LANZAMIENTO, CUSTOMER JOURNEY Y EXPERIENCIA DE MARCA

TOOL 1 · WHY WE?
SIMPLICIDAD COMO EXPERIENCIA

TOOL 2 · BRAND NARRATIVES
¿CUENTAS BIEN LO QUE SE TE DA BIEN?

TOOL 3 · BRAND RITUALS
SUBLIMEMENTE TANGIBLE LO INTANGIBLE

TOOL 4 · THE 10 GOLDEN MOMENTS
HAY DOS CAMINOS: TU COMPETENCIA O TÚ

TOOL 5 · THE BURN PYRAMID
MARCAR A FUEGO

BENEFICIOS DE ACTIVAR EL DRIVER:

- Clarificar tu propuesta en todo el customer journey
- Empoderar a tus audiencia interna y externa
- Crear rituales de marca
- Conocer y activar los 10 momentos de oro
- Potenciar todas las etapas de relación con tus clientes
- Crear un lanzamiento y experiencia de marca memorable
- Innovar e impactar con significado
- Transcender y crear una propuesta impactante e inolvidable

WHY WE?

SIMPLICIDAD COMO EXPERIENCIA FLUYE

LOS CONSUMIDORES SON LÍQUIDOS, FLUYEN POR EL CAMINO EN EL QUE MENOS OPOSICIÓN ENCUENTREN

LA SIMPLICIDAD COMO EXPERIENCIA DE VALOR. SON COMO EL AGUA. PONLES LAS COSAS FÁCILES PARA QUE TE NAVEGUEN HACIA TI

¿Qué es?

Catarsis, has roto el cascarón. Bienvenido al Mundo. Ahora que te has lanzado al mercado ya no estás solo, estás rodeado de competencia, buena, bonita y quizás barata.

Tus clientes están sobresaturados de opciones y son infieles e impacientes. Haz que entiendan de una forma sencilla qué eres para ellos, qué beneficio pueden obtener gracias a ti y cómo pueden tener acceso a él. Enamora rápido, la atención se dispersa.

¿Por qué es importante?

Ponle las cosas fáciles a tu cliente, habla su idioma, simplifica su experiencia y facilita su vida. Dales más valor pero menos trabajo. Expresa de manera clara por qué eres la mejor opción.

En un entorno híper competitivo debes dejar claro por qué deben comprarte a ti y no a tu competencia.

Sedúceles sin darles pereza.

MEET THE TOOL ——————————

Recibimos más de 6.000 impactos publicitarios diarios, lo que supone uno cada 10 segundos. En muy poco tiempo tienes que dar respuesta de forma muy clara y concisa a estas tres preguntas:

1. ¿Qué problema resuelves?
2. ¿Qué te hace ser la mejor opción?
3. ¿Cuál es tu llamada a la acción?

Fíjate en las descripciones de tus competidores en Google. Te enseñarán de forma sencilla como están atrayendo la atención de sus clientes. Algún ejemplo que podemos encontrar:

Glovo

Glovo - Tu ciudad a domicilio - Entregas en minutos. Descubre tu nuevo restaurante o tienda favorita, pide lo que quieras y te lo llevamos. Los restaurantes y tiendas de tu ciudad siguen abiertos. Pide a domicilio con Glovo.

NIKE

NIKE: zapatillas, ropa y más - Entregas y devoluciones gratis. Compra las últimas novedades para tenis, fútbol y otros deportes en NIKE.com. Da lo mejor de ti en cualquier momento y lugar con la ropa y las zapatillas Nike.

Uber

Gana dinero conduciendo o pide un viaje ahora en España Consigue un viaje en unos minutos. O conviértete en conductor y gana dinero con tu propio horario. Uber te ofrece mejores formas de moverte, trabajar y...

Visto en mayo 2022

WHY WE?

¿QUÉ PROBLEMA
RESUELVES
A TU CLIENTE?

¿QUÉ TE HACE
SER LA MEJOR
OPCIÓN?

¿CUÁL ES TU
LLAMADA A LA
ACCIÓN?

PLAY THE TOOL

¿Qué problema
resuelves a tu cliente? ———————

¿Qué te hace ser
la mejor opción? ———————

¿Cuál es tu llamada
a la acción? ———————

WHY WE?

BRAND
NARRATIVES

CUÉNTAME UN CUENTO, HAZME VIVIR UNA HISTORIA

REDUCE EL GAP ENTRE LO QUE ERES Y LO QUE PARECES

Las marcas tienen mucho que contar, pero es importante que lo hagamos de una forma estructurada que clarifique el mensaje, aporte el mayor valor posible y nos posicione de la forma más competitiva. Comunicamos básicamente para que nos identifiquen con lo que deseamos.

Una narrativa coherente busca disminuir el *gap* entre nuestra identidad de marca y nuestra imagen. Lo que somos versus lo que parecemos. Para ello contamos con diferentes temáticas de contenido que repetiremos para que nuestro mensaje cale. Estos grupos de contenidos estratégicos los llamo sagas.

El coche sueco, el coche seguro

Es importante que a la hora de comunicar no soltemos cañonazos con mucha información inconexa y variopinta. Eso solo saturará y confundirá a tus audiencias, y te hará perder tu posicionamiento, dispersándolo en direcciones que no aportan competitividad.

Es más beneficioso que nuestras audiencias tengan claro 3 o 4 grades conceptos que interiorizar -sagas- donde ubicarnos de forma rápida.

Por ejemplo, si pienso en seguridad en automoción rápidamente pienso en Volvo. Esto es gracias a todos los impactos que me han ido llegando a lo largo de los años. También al pensar en Volvo pienso -por ejemplo- en diseño y en Suecia. Podríamos decir que estas son sus 3 sagas bien trabajadas a lo largo del tiempo.

Pero ¿qué pasaría si Volvo no cumpliera su promesa de seguridad?, ¿o que sus coches no estuvieran diseñados en Suecia? Perdería toda nuestra confianza. -Esto es vital, ya que además de parecerlo hay que serlo-. Además de las sagas tenemos que comunicar nuestros puntos de prueba que demuestran que lo que decimos es cierto.

Crea una narrativa clara y tangible. Pasa del *storytelling* al *storydoing*. De contar a desarrollar. De hablar a activar.

IDENTIFICACIÓN + ADMIRACIÓN = LOVE BRAND

MEET THE TOOL ───────────────

Pasamos de historias a hechos. Refutamos nuestros storytelling con una narrativa coherente y consistente.

Aquí las partes claves de esta tool

>>Sigamos con el ejemplo de Volvo para ilustrar la herramienta.

1. LOS RELATOS:

Dos relatos, dos oportunidades: nacidos en un garaje.

Tenemos que ser relevantes para nuestras audiencias externas pero también internas.

Cuando pensamos en un garaje nos vienen a la cabeza los inicios de grandes compañías. Todos sabemos que allí nació Microsoft, Google o Amazon. Pero ¿saben tus empleados cuál es el relato interno de la creación de la compañía donde trabajan? ¿De qué hechos deberían estar orgullosos?

1.1 RELATO INTERNO: Nuestros empleados son nuestros mejores embajadores. Es importante que ellos conozcan nuestra narrativa para que puedan defenderla con orgullo.

¿Tienes clara tu historia personal como marca?

1.2. RELATO EXTERNO: Las grandes ideas y temáticas que queremos posicionar en la mente de nuestros *stakeholders* (clientes, proveedores, gobiernos, competencia, aliados...)

Lo que buscamos que conozcan de nosotros y con lo qué queremos ser identificados.

BRAND NARRATIVES & SAGAS

2. LAS SAGAS

Las sagas son las grandes temáticas a tratar. Es importante que sean temas muy fáciles de identificar y comprender. Propuestas cuanto más claras mejor.

Por ejemplo -volviendo a Volvo- podríamos identificar 3 sagas dentro de su relato externo:

1. El coche más seguro
2. Calidad Sueca
3. El coche familiar

Como sagas del relato interno podríamos proponer:

1. De rodamientos a referentes
2. Innovación como cultura
3. Somos responsables con nuestros bosques

3. PROOF POINTS: TUS AVALES O PUNTOS DE ANCLAJE

¿Qué datos reales avalan tus sagas?¿Qué es lo que hace que lo que cuentas sea real? ¿Qué sostiene tu propuesta? ¿Qué datos cualitativos y cuantitativos hacen que seas el coche más seguro?

Si por ejemplo eres defensor de los bosques suecos, ¿qué haces para manteneros con vida?

4. ACCIONES

Activando y tangibilizando nuestras sagas a través de hechos. No es solo lo que dices, sino lo que haces. Una vez comprendida la saga y los puntos de anclaje es el momento de activar y dar vida.

¿Dónde y cómo estás comunicado lo que eres? ¿Qué acciones están tangibilizando tu historia? ¿Cómo haces real y palpable el valor que aportas? ¿Cómo se están enterando tus audiencias de todo lo que haces bien?

PLAY THE TOOL

NARRATIVAS

RELATO INTERNO

SAGA 1	SAGA 2

PUNTOS DE ANCLAJE	PUNTOS DE ANCLAJE

ACCIONES	ACCIONES

¿Qué quieres que conozcan y valoren de tu marca?

RELATO EXTERNO

SAGA 1	SAGA 2

PUNTOS DE ANCLAJE	PUNTOS DE ANCLAJE

ACCIONES	ACCIONES

BRAND NARAATIVES & SAGAS

BRAND
RITUALS

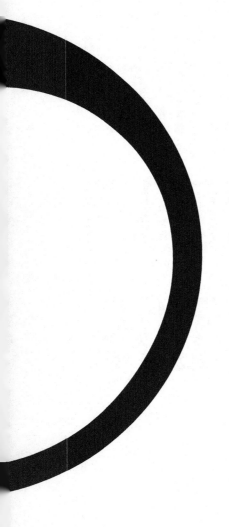

CONTROLADORES Y HEDONISTAS. HAZME ADICTA A TUS PRESAGIOS.

HACIENDO TANGIBLE LO INTANGIBLE.
CAPITALIZANDO NUESTRO EQUITY

Las marcas están compuestas por un conjunto de asociaciones y símbolos intangibles, pero también de acciones y rituales muy tangibles. Experiencias que al interactuar con la marca se repiten siempre.

¿Qué es?
Una palabra que me encanta del español es presagio -literalmente significa señal o indicio que se interpreta como el anuncio de un hecho futuro- y de esto justo, va esta herramienta.

Cuando vas a Starbucks sabes qué experiencias y rituales vas a vivir allí. La marca está por todas partes, la vives, la sientes y la tocas. Sabes que nada más entrar las cosas van a estar como siempre -independientemente de si entras a uno en París o en Madrid- el olor a café, la decoración de madera, los sofás y las mesitas... También sabes que al pedir un café un empleado con un mandil verde va a poner tu nombre en tu vaso.

Vivimos patrones que se repiten, ritualizados. Experiencias tangibles y actos que marcan la diferencia de forma sutil.

¿Por qué es importante?
Somos animales de costumbres. Nos gusta que nos sorprendan pero también nos encanta tener el control de la cotidianidad. Potencia todas las acciones, costumbres y rituales que aporten valor a tu cliente y hagan que se fidelice.

NOS GUSTA QUE NOS TRATEN BIEN Y NOS HAGAN SENTIR ESPECIALES.
PERO NOS GUSTA MÁS SABER QUE ESTO VA A PASAR.

MEET THE TOOL ───────────────

Ritualiza todas las interacciones de tu marca con tu público. Crea ceremonias propias valiosas. Maximiza tus oportunidades de impacto y sorprende, siempre. Hazle vivir algo único.

TRES MOMENTOS

1. IN

Son todas las acciones ritualizadas que recibe tu cliente al entrar en contacto directo con tu marca o servicio. La primera impresión. Ej. El Starbucks de Lima es igual que el de París, te saludan por tu nombre gracias a tu tarjeta de fidelización...

2. DURING

Es todo lo que sucede en el momento **justo** de la experiencia. Mientas la vives. Durante la interacción a tiempo real.
Ej. Te ofrecen el Frapuchino sabor Navidad que solo está esta semana, al pedirlo escriben tu nombre en el vaso...

3. OUT

El todo lo que sucede fuera del momento de consumo. Aquellos rituales que le impactan aunque no esté presente ni en contacto directo con la marca
Ej. La marca te felicita por tu cumpleaños, la newsletter de los viernes con novedades, directo en RRSS desde las plantaciones de café que ve desde su casa...

BRAND RITUALS

DOS RITUALES

1. ACCIONES INDIRECTAS O AMBIENTALES

Aquello que percibe como ritual icónico repetitivo pero que no se aplica exclusivamente a él.

Ej. El olor a café recién molido de Starbucks.

2. ACCIONES DIRECTAS O PERSONALES

Rituales que le repercuten y afectan personalmente.

Ej. Cuando ponen su nombre en el vaso de café.

PLAY THE TOOL

Momentos

IN

DURING

OUT

Rituales

ACCIONES
INDIRECTAS
AMBIENTALES

ACCIONES
DIRECTAS
PERSONALES

THE BRAND RITUALS

THE 10 GOLD MOMENTS
CUSTOMER
JOURNEY

Ratatouille es una rata

PON LA MÚSICA QUE NECESITA EN CADA MOMENTO

Este *customer journey* mapea los 10 momentos de oro de cualquier proceso de compra.

Son las 10 etapas que harán que tu cliente siga el camino hacia una relación con tu marca o que te abandone para siempre.

Cada momento de oro es decisivo. Si todo va bien, tu cliente continuará el viaje de tu mano y hará negocios contigo. Si las cosas salen mal y no cumples con sus expectativas se irá a otra parte, te abandonará para siempre y te dejará metido en la ratonera del mercado. Recuerda: cada momento es un tesoro -oro puro- para aportar valor y diferenciación a tus clientes.

Haz que fluyan hacia ti.

¿Qué es?
No hay una segunda oportunidad para una primera impresión.

Antes de cerrar una venta, tu cliente, ya ha pasado por 5 momentos de oro. En este *costumer journey*, cada momento es decisivo. Solo hay dos direcciones posibles: hacía tí o hacia tu competencia.

¿Por qué es importante?
En cada momento el consumidor necesita diferentes pruebas o motivaciones para seguir su camino. Debemos analizar qué paracaídas necesita para poder pasar de un momento a otro de la forma más eficiente.

Y recuerda, si la cagas aprovecha para darle la vuelta. Ratatouille era una rata. Pero ¡tremenda rata!

MEET THE TOOL

LOS 10 MOMENTOS DE ORO:

 ZERO BITS (ZB) - EL NACIMIENTO DE LA NECESIDAD

El momento cero o instante en que el usuario decide hacerse con un producto o servicio. Es el momento donde se desencadena el *trigger* y aparece una nueva necesidad, innata o condicionada por una acción de marketing. La persona busca satisfacer esa nueva necesidad y en este contexto no existen marcas, solo soluciones. Esta etapa se compone de dos momentos clave:

MOMENTO 1 - AWARENESS/CONCIENCIA

Es importante que sepamos qué desencadenantes provocamos y en qué puntos de contacto estamos impactando y creando consciencia de nuestra marca. Si no saben que existimos es imposible que nos deseen.

MOMENTO 2 - INTERÉS

El usuario empieza a plantearse beneficios personales sobre esta nueva necesidad o idea. Analiza, absorbe, se empapa de razones para pasar al siguiente momento.

 ACTIVE BITS (AB) - BÚSQUEDA ACTIVA DE LO QUE ES MEJOR PARA ÉL

El cliente pasa a la acción, toma un rol activo y empieza a buscar información acerca de lo que quiere -lee *blogs, reviews,* opiniones- se encuentra en una fase *commodity* y busca la mejor solución a su necesidad. En esta parte es fundamental que encuentre una solución que satisfaga sus necesidades de forma óptima.

MOMENTO 3- CONSIDERACIÓN

Analiza si de verdad será beneficioso para él la compra. Refuta ideas, comprueba teorías y analiza su mejor opción para saber si le compensa seguir adelante con la compra y respectiva inversión o es mejor abandonar esta idea. ¿Le aportará beneficios que compensen el coste? Aquí es importante que expongamos y hablemos del valor del producto más allá del precio. *Value for money.*

MOMENTO 4 - EVALUACIÓN

Ha decidido que le compensa la inversión. En esta etapa analiza diferentes proveedores para ver cuál será el que mejor satisfacerá su necesidad. En este momento necesita pruebas de que cumplirás tu promesa. Lee a otros compradores, pide información, contrasta con amigos... Para saber si es la opción correcta y fiable.

 TRUST BITS (TB) - TE ELIGE, CONFÍA Y TE COMPRA

Cuando el consumidor se encuentra con el producto y decide comprar. Es el momento en el que se ha decidido por una marca y pasa a la acción. Es importante que le pongamos fácil este paso para que pueda realizar la transacción sin dificultad.

THE 10 GOLDEN MOMENTS

MOMENTO 5 - DECISIÓN

El usuario quiere tu producto o servicio, se ha decidido por ti, pero la compra aún no está hecha. Es importante que motives a la acción y que le pongas las cosas fáciles.

MOMENTO 6 - COMPRA

¿Es sencillo comprarte? ¿Qué pasos tiene que hacer tu nuevo cliente para finalizar con éxito la transacción? Es el momento donde le tienes que dar seguridad y facilidades. Que culmine la transacción.

 ### WIN BITS (WB) - CONFIRMA QUE CUMPLES TUS PROMESAS. HA ACERTADO.

Cuando el consumidor empieza a usar el producto. Si todo va bien, sus expectativas se confirmarán y esto dará lugar a una relación a largo plazo.

MOMENTO 7- EXPECTATIVAS

El famoso unboxing. Cuando por fin se topa con tu producto o servicio entre sus manos. Este momento es crucial, además de cumplir sus expectativas tienes la posibilidad de superarlas con servicios añadidos o con momentos dulces inesperados.

MOMENTO 8 - REPETICIÓN

Un cliente contento es un cliente fiel. Buscamos que la próxima vez que tenga esta misma necesidad sea leal a nuestra marca. Que repita la experiencia y vuelva una y otra vez a nosotros. Por eso es fundamental crear una relación de total confianza con él. Nútrele y estate presente en su día a día.

 ### SOCIAL BITS (SB) - FARDA DE TI CON ORGULLO. LE REPRESENTAS.

Las expectativas han sido superadas y se siente orgulloso de su compra. Representas valores que él quiere comunicar de sí mismo. Por eso, será fiel y recomendará tu marca como propia.

MOMENTO 9 - LEALTAD

Te elegirá a ti aunque tu competencia le ofrezca mejores condiciones. Esto es por los valores emocionales más allá de los funcionales que le ofreces, o por lo que significas para él. Activa tus motivaciones emocionales en este punto para mantener su amor y compromiso con tu marca.

MOMENTO 10 - RECOMENDACIÓN

Tus clientes son tus mejores vendedores. Cuando un cliente esté orgulloso de consumir tu marca querrá fardar de ello. Analiza qué sienten gracias a ti y qué les das para que ellos puedan compartirte, recomendarte y exponerte de la mejor forma posible.

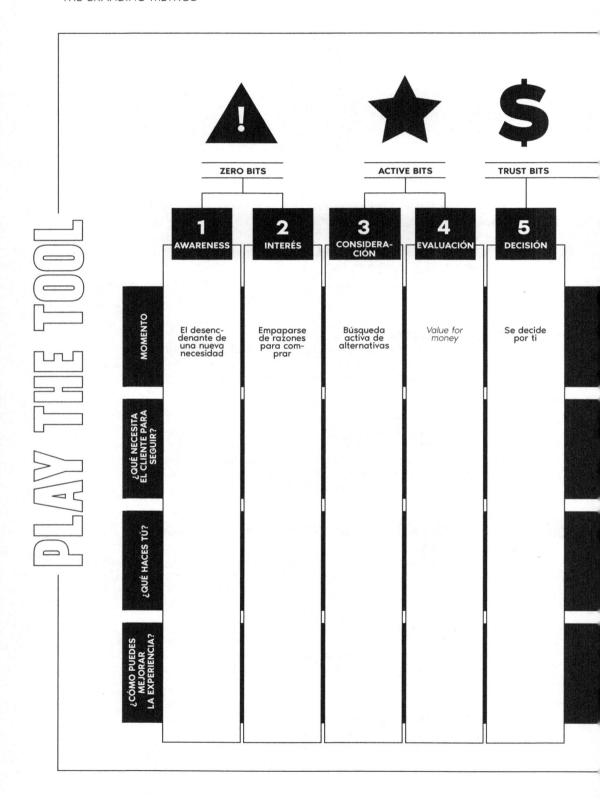

PLAY THE TOOL

ZERO BITS

ACTIVE BITS

TRUST BITS

1 AWARENESS

2 INTERÉS

3 CONSIDERA-CIÓN

4 EVALUACIÓN

5 DECISIÓN

| MOMENTO | El desenc-denante de una nueva necesidad | Empaparse de razones para com-prar | Búsqueda activa de alternativas | *Value for money* | Se decide por ti |

¿QUÉ NECESITA EL CLIENTE PARA SEGUIR?

¿QUÉ HACES TÚ?

¿CÓMO PUEDES MEJORAR LA EXPERIENCIA?

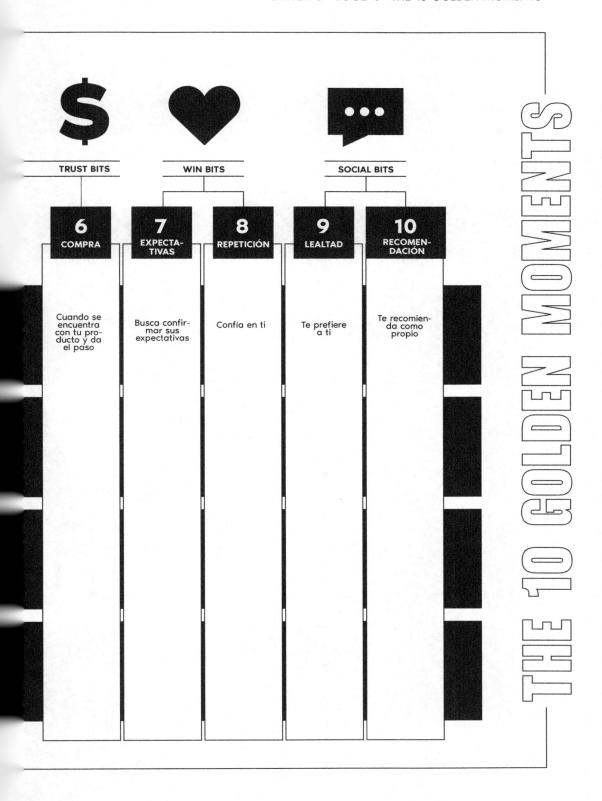

THE BURN

HACER LAS COSAS BIEN SE DA POR HECHO

SI TU VALOR MÁS DIFERENCIADOR ES LA INNOVACIÓN ES QUE TE FALTA MUCHA INNOVACIÓN. CUANDO UNA EXPERIENCIA ES WOW ES TODO MENOS WOW

¿Qué es?

Te presento mi pirámide de transcendencia, te guiará para que puedas definir acciones y experiencias que de verdad importen e impacten a tus clientes. Siguiendo las 6 etapas de relación con ellos.

Pasa de ser un commodity a una elección directa

Hacer las cosas bien se da por hecho. Que tu marca tenga una identidad cuidada, un envío a tiempo y una web usable es un higiénico -basic- del mercado. Si no lo tuvieras, no estarías en el juego.

La palabra *brand* -marca- tiene su origen de *burn* -quemar/marcar- básicamente seguimos identificando a nuestro ganado pero de una forma más sutil. Las marcas han evolucionado y ahora además de marcar productos o propiedades tienen un valor activo en nuestra sociedad. Expresamos quienes somos a través del simbolismo colectivo y significados que catalizamos a través de ellas.

Por eso, una verdadera experiencia inolvidable -irrepetible- es *BURN*, algo que te quema, que se te tatúa en la piel como una marca a fuego. No la vas a olvidar. No vas a poder dejar de hablar de ella. No vas a poder dejar de compartirla. No es solamente guay.

Represéntame y te compartiré. Benefíciame y te compraré

Nuestras relaciones con las marcas y con la sociedad están en continua transformación, por eso, para importar a las personas hay que ser cada vez más astuto e intrépido pero sin olvidar ser coherente y elocuente.

Aprovecha y desarrolla todas las oportunidades de activación. Ahora más que nunca, hay que hacer las cosas de forma diferente. Hoy, solo los más ágiles, certeros y valientes, seguirán siendo relevantes.

MEET THE TOOL

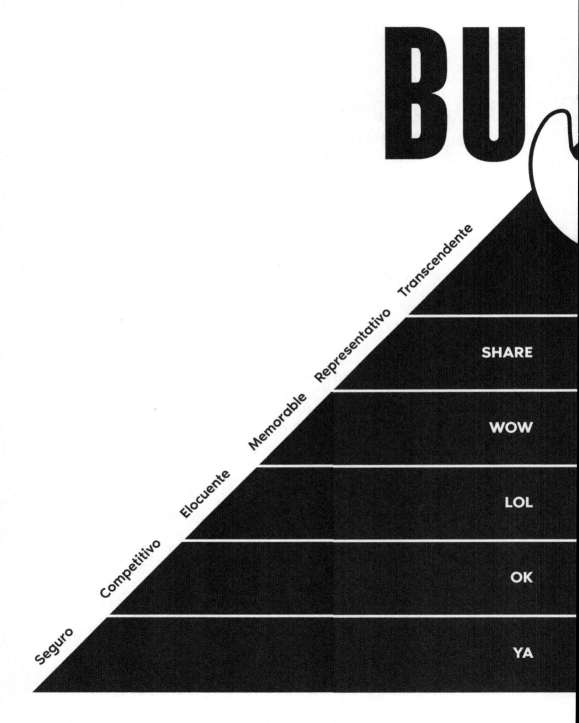

SHARE

WOW

LOL

OK

YA

Transcendente

Representativo

Memorable

Elocuente

Competitivo

Seguro

THE BURN PYRAMID

RN

¿Qué le haces ser?
¿Qué acciones estás haciendo que le hayan dejado sin palabras?

¿Qué defiende o expone gracias a ti ?
¿Qué acciones estás haciendo que quiera compartir?

¿Haces vivir algo extraordinario a tu cliente?
¿Qué acciones estás haciendo diferenciales?

¿Tienes una personalidad definida y notoria?
¿Tienes carácter?
¿Qué acciones estás haciendo divertidas e interesantes?

¿Qué acciones te hacen diferente de la competencia?
¿Qué acciones estás haciendo bien?

¿Qué acciones estás haciendo basic?
¿Qué elementos valorados por el mercado aportas?

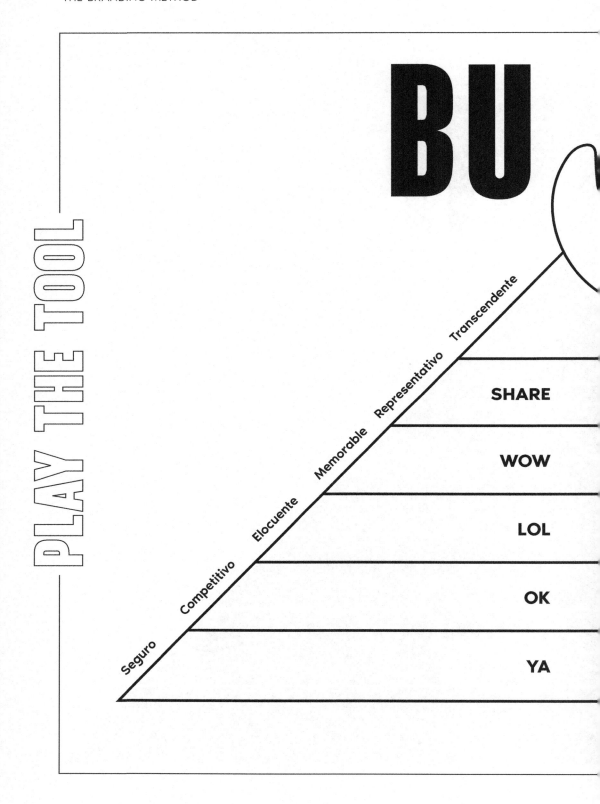

PLAY THE TOOL

BU

Seguro · Competitivo · Elocuente · Memorable · Representativo · Transcendente

SHARE

WOW

LOL

OK

YA

THE BURN PYRAMID

¿Y AHO

RA QUÉ?

¡PUES A VOLAR!
¿Y SI SALE MAL? Y SI SALE BIEN, ¿QUÉ?

Entrégate a tu proyecto pero no te enamores de él.

Siempre que me da miedo empezar algo relativizo. El suelo es un duro cero, sé dónde está y dónde puedo terminar si las cosas no salen como quiero. Lo peor que puede pasar es que vuelva al punto de partida. En cambio, el cielo es infinito y lleno de posibilidades. No tiene límite, es apasionante.

Tienes el mapa. Tienes las herramientas. Tienes la voluntad. Ahora te toca salir a jugar tus cartas. Innova y lanza tu visión.

Prueba, ajusta, cambia, transfórmate. Atrévete o trabajarás para los osados que lo hicieron.

Nunca es un buen momento, siempre es un buen momento. Haz lo que quieras. Haz lo que quieres.

Ahora y siempre.

HAZ LO QUE QUIERAS. HAZ LO QUE QUIERES.

MEET THE FULL BRANDING TOOL

POR QUÉ HACES LO QUE HACES
Y SOBRE TODO PARA QUÉ

PROPÓSITO
¿Por qué haces del Mundo
un lugar mejor?

**CAUSA
JUSTA**
¿Por qué estás
en el juego?

VALORES
¿Qué predicas?

PERSONALIDAD
¿Cómo te relacionas
con tu entorno?

POSICIONAMIENTO
¿Qué te hace valioso
frente a los otros?

**BRAND
POWER**

PROMESA
¿Qué van a vivir
gracias a ti?

**UNIQUE SELLING
PROPOSITION**
¿Qué te
hace único?

REASON TO BELIEVE
¿Qué te avala?

THE BRAND POWER

Certifícate como consultor oficial en
THE BRANDING METHOD

DESCARGA AQUÍ TU CANVAS
IMPRIMIBLE CON TODA TU ESTRATEGIA

CONSIGUE MÁS TOOLS, FORMACIÓN Y METODOLOGÍA EN

www.padawanbranding.com

Comparte tu proceso creativo con la comunidad brander en:

 CAROLINA KAIROS    @LADYBRANDING    @THEBRANDINGMETHOD_BOOK

"Les meilleures choses dans la vie sont gratuites.

Les deuxièmes meilleures choses sont très, très chères."

"Las mejores cosas de la vida son gratis.
Las segundas mejores, son muy, muy caras."

Gabrielle Chanel ᗡC

Con esta frase terminé mi trabajo fin de Máster de Branding hace casi 10 años. Hoy vuelvo a terminar con lo mismo.

Las mejores cosas de la vida son gratis - es más, no tienen precio porque no se pueden comprar-. En cambio, las segundas mejores son muy caras.

Ha sido un placer y recuerda: nunca confundas valor con precio.

Suerte en el amor y en ser amado que es el verdadero privilegio excepcional. Que tu negocio triunfe es más ordinario.

Negocios hay muchos y por todas partes.

Carolina Kairos

FUN;

Printed in Great Britain
by Amazon